SEASONAL ENTERTAINING

SEASONAL ENTERTAINING

Sheridan Rogers

Styled by Robin Duffecy
Photography by Rodney Weidland

CASSELL

A CASSELL BOOK

First published in the United Kingdom 1993 by
Cassell
Villiers House
41/47 Strand
London WC2N 5JE

First published in Australia in 1993
by Angus&Robertson*Publishers* Pty Limited
A division of HarperCollins*Publishers* (Australia) Pty Limited
25 Ryde Road, Pymble, Sydney NSW 2073, Australia

British Library Cataloguing-in-Publication Data:
A catalogue record for this book is available from the British Library.
ISBN 0 304 34335 8

Printed in Hong Kong

In memory of Robin Duffecy,
and for her children, Matilda and Jim.

And fruits: I will buy fruits, and in their sweetness

that country's earth and sky will live again.

For that is what you understood: ripe fruits.

You set them before the canvas, in white bowls,

and weighed out each one's heaviness with your colours.

Women too, you saw, were fruits; and children, moulded

from inside, into the shapes of their existence.

~

RAINER MARIA RILKE, REQUIEM

ACKNOWLEDGMENTS

I would like to acknowledge the assistance of the following people and organisations:
Sandra Rigby; Polly Birks; John Duffecy; Cherise Koch; Margaret Connolly; Kim Anderson; Connie Simon, Eastside Providores; Michael Keenan, Tamlaght Orchard; Teresa Somma, Paesanella Cheese Factory; Mark Armstrong, Armstrong's Restaurant; Colleen Johnson, Galway Downs; Marieke Brugman, Howqua Dale Gourmet Retreat; Neil Perry, Rockpool Restaurant; Diana Wassall; John Wilson, Mohr Foods; Australian Horticultural Corporation; Paddington Fruit Markets; Appley Hoare Antiques and The Bay Tree.

Finally I would also like to thank Jerry Rogers, Sharne and Rodney Weidland, Steven Adey for lending us his beautiful garden to photograph, Victoria Alexander for her generosity in lending us her beautiful restaurant 'The Bather's Pavilion' for some of the photography, Damien Pignolet of Claude's Restaurant and Bistro Moncur at The Woollahra Hotel for his ideas, inspiration and generosity, Millie Sherman of 'I Piatti', and Ralph Potter, chef at Lilianfels, for sharing his recipes and ideas.

CONTENTS

AUTUMN 82

~

WINTER 116

~

INTRODUCTION

When it starts raining mangoes, I know it's summer. At my family's farm in sub-tropical Queensland, the old mango trees drop their bounty at the height of summer. Often the mangoes fall by themselves, other times they're helped along by a peacock or flying fox. It can be quite a shock to be hit by one, especially when you're lazing there, under the canopy, out of the sun. It's also very pleasurable to pick one up, peel it and taste its delicious flavour and texture.

Summer is one of my favourite seasons. Long, lazy afternoons when the family retire for a siesta (that's if we haven't been knocked out by a falling mango) to recover from the heat. Golden days filled with the sound of crickets singing their hallelujah chorus, platters of watermelon wedges, picnics and barbecues and endless swimming at the beach; long, cool drinks, tennis, cold buffets on the terrace and late storms. Days when we like to eat simple, tasty food which doesn't require too much time in the kitchen. Days which remind us of how good it is to be alive.

And then autumn — not just all the dawns of autumn, nor the shorter, cooler days, but the evenings as well. Soft, sad evenings when shadows are lengthening and leaves beginning their transformations through gold, red and yellow to brown. I love the rustling as they fall and the sudden gusts of wind and dust. There is a wistful, mellow feeling in the air during autumn which makes us pause and take stock, beckoning us to reflect a little on our lives. Mornings when it is good to go mushrooming, and pick figs; to invite friends over for a long breakfast; and to experiment with some new dishes in the kitchen using some of the tawny autumn

fruits — the pears and pomegranates, grapes and crabapples.

When winter finally arrives with its cold, crisp days, we turn indoors and back to the hearth — to solid earthy foods which fill and sustain, to reading and entertaining at home, to games of scrabble and chess, to log fires and bowls of steaming soup. I like to cook a lot in winter, to fill the house with inviting aromas like casseroles and roasts and marmalade.

And who doesn't look forward to spring? To the sight of the first green buds pushing their way through the earth; to the songs of the birds, their celebration of life and confirmation that the cycle is about to begin again; to strawberries and asparagus, new peas and fresh tarragon.

Discovering and celebrating seasonal produce is a way of becoming more attuned to nature; of being aware, as our ancestors were, of the rhythms of the planet. From the earliest times, the seasons shaped almost every aspect of man's life. Different communities divided up the year differently. In rice-growing countries, for example, the seasons were divided according to the state of growth of the crop. The ancient Egyptians recognised only three seasons — rainy, cold and warm. Some societies had no calendar, depending on the appearance of certain stars, animal and bird migrations and changes in specific weather patterns to measure the passage of time.

The importance of the great birth-death-rebirth drama was recognised in festivals, powerful myths and legends, and personified in gods and goddesses. Perhaps one of the most haunting myths is that of Persephone,

Left: Pomegranates.

11

daughter of Demeter, the earth mother. Persephone was abducted by the king of the underworld, Hades. In her despair at the loss of her daughter, Demeter neglected the fertility of the earth and Zeus was forced to intervene, demanding that Hades return Persephone to her mother. But because Persephone had eaten a pomegranate seed from the underworld, she was condemned to return to Hades's kingdom for at least part of the year, during which time her mother, in her sorrow, would allow the earth to lie barren and infertile.

In all of this I am reminded of a pop song by The Byrds, 'Turn, Turn, Turn'; the one to do with the seasons — the seasons of man, and of life. I remember the first time I heard it and the mixed feelings I had as I listened. It was only later I discovered this successful pop song was based on a passage from Ecclesiastes (3: 1–8). For all his doom and gloom, the preacher had expressed something profound and beautiful:

'To everything there is a season, and a time to every purpose under the heaven: A time to be born, and a time to die; a time to plant, and a time to pluck that

Left: Fresh spring peas.

which is planted . . . A time to weep, and a time to laugh; a time to mourn and a time to dance . . .'

The passage is, of course, about more than just the passing of the agricultural seasons. It is about appropriateness (that is, that there is a time for everything) and it also refers to the seasons of man ('a time to be born and a time to die').

Working on this book, the words of the passage came back to me in more ways than one. As we gave birth to this new creation, we were also participating in a death. When we first started work, I knew that my friend, stylist Robin Duffecy, had breast cancer. The cancer had moved into her bones, but she was still well enough to work. In fact, she was determined to keep working, much to the concern of her husband, John. Her tenacity and determination were something to behold. The challenge of doing the book was, in some mysterious way, keeping her alive. When, towards the end, the cancer had moved into her liver, there were days when she could barely lift an arm, let alone stand to have a final look at a shot through the camera. Yet there she would be morning after morning, immaculately groomed and dressed, sitting on the sofa in her kitchen, waiting for us to begin the day.

We were half-way through completing *Seasonal Entertaining* when she died.

This book is a tribute to Robin, to her courage and determination, and finally to her graciousness, reflected, as you can see, in the pages of this beautiful book.

I could not have finished it without the help of another dear friend and colleague, photographer Rodney Weidland. Rodney's skill as a food photographer, his gentle, kindly demeanour and painterly eye have been invaluable. Polly Birks, John Duffecy, Cherise Koch, Margaret Connolly, Victoria Alexander, Damien Pignolet and Appley Hoare were also of great assistance.

SPRING

MENU

A Spring Breakfast

Spring can be a mixture of cool, wintry days and warmer, balmier weather. This menu combines hearty crepes and hash browns with refreshing spring fruits — honeydew melon and strawberries — to complement the transitional new season.

BUCKWHEAT CREPES WITH FRESH STRAWBERRY PRESERVE, NATURAL (PLAIN) YOGHURT AND BROWN SUGAR

~

HASH BROWNS WITH BACON AND GRILLED (BROILED) TOMATO

~

FRENCH TARRAGON OMELETTE, HONEYDEW MELON AND GRAPEFRUIT JUICE

~

FRESH STRAWBERRIES WITH FROMAGE BLANC AND BREAD

~

BABY CAMEMBERTS

Serves 6–8

BUCKWHEAT CREPES WITH FRESH STRAWBERRY PRESERVE, NATURAL (PLAIN) YOGHURT AND BROWN SUGAR

INGREDIENTS

1¼ cups (150 g, 5 oz) plain (all-purpose) flour

~

¾ cup (100 g, 3½ oz) buckwheat flour

~

1 teaspoon salt

~

¼ cup (50 g, 1½ oz) caster (superfine) sugar

~

4 eggs, lightly beaten

~

2 cups (500 mls, 17 fl oz) milk

~

3 teaspoons melted butter

~

500 g (1 lb) fresh strawberries

~

approximately 2 cups (500 mls, 17 fl oz) natural (plain) yoghurt

~

brown (soft, light brown) sugar or light muscovado sugar for sprinkling

Sift the dry ingredients together into a bowl. Make a well in the centre and add the eggs and milk. Beat well, then add the butter, stirring thoroughly to combine. Cover and let stand 1 hour. Strain the mixture to ensure it is free of lumps.

To make the crepes, heat a little butter in a crepe pan, pouring off any excess. Use a jug (pitcher) and pour a little of the mixture onto the bottom of the pan, rotating it quickly to coat the bottom thinly and evenly. Pour out any excess batter. When small bubbles appear, turn the crepe over and cook the other side for about 1 minute.

Serve the crepes with the fresh strawberries, roughly chopped in a food processor, and a generous spoonful of natural yoghurt sprinkled with the sugar.

Makes about 20 crepes

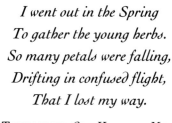

I went out in the Spring
To gather the young herbs.
So many petals were falling,
Drifting in confused flight,
That I lost my way.

KI NO TSURAYUKI, *ONE HUNDRED MORE POEMS*
FROM THE JAPANESE

Previous page: Fresh Strawberries, Fromage Blanc and French Bread.
Right: Buckwheat Crepes with Strawberry Preserve and Yoghurt.

HASH BROWNS

INGREDIENTS

8 medium waxy (all-purpose) potatoes, peeled

~

150 g (5 oz) clarified butter

~

salt and pepper

~

6–8 bacon rashers (slices)

~

3–4 ripe tomatoes, cut in halves

Boil the potatoes in plenty of rapidly boiling salted water for 5 minutes. Remove and refresh under cold water.

Heat a quarter of the butter in a heavy-based pan. While this is heating, coarsely grate half the potatoes and dry them with a teatowel (dishcloth). Do this quickly so that they don't start to discolour. Press the grated potatoes into the pan, season with salt and freshly ground black pepper. Cook evenly until a crust begins to form. Remove from the heat, cover with a lid and let the potatoes steam a little to cook through. Return to the heat and, with a spatula, flip the potatoes over, adding more clarified butter as you do so. Cook until golden and tender on the other side. Remove from the pan and keep warm. Repeat procedure with the remaining potatoes.

Meanwhile, in another pan, cook the bacon until crispy and fry the tomatoes until heated through. Alternatively cook these under a hot grill (broiler). To serve, cut the hash browns into thirds or quarters.

FRENCH TARRAGON OMELETTE

FRESH FRENCH TARRAGON IS AVAILABLE IN
SPRING AND COMBINES WONDERFULLY WITH EGGS.

INGREDIENTS

PER PERSON

3 fresh eggs

~

1 tablespoon water

~

1 tablespoon fresh French tarragon, chopped (or to taste)

~

salt and pepper

~

knob of butter

With a fork, whisk the eggs together with the water. Add the tarragon and a pinch of salt and pepper and whisk well.

Put the knob of butter into a frying pan (skillet) and when it is foaming, pour in the eggs, tilting the pan and moving it around. With a fork, keep lifting the cooked eggs around the edge so that the runny part in the centre moves under the part that has set. Repeat until the eggs have set underneath but are still creamy and a little runny on top. Fold a third of the omelette towards the centre and roll out onto a warmed plate, tilting the pan so that the omelette folds over again. Serve immediately.

Left: Hash Browns with Bacon and Grilled (Broiled) Tomato.

HONEYDEW MELON

What could make a more refreshing start to the day than slices of juicy, delicious honeydew melon? These melons are available almost all year round. Select those which give off a sweet smell at the stalk end. They should have a good colour and unblemished skin.

GRAPEFRUIT JUICE

Grapefruits are an excellent source of vitamin C and make a good drink with which to begin the day. Choose fruit which is evenly coloured without brown or soft patches.

Left: French Tarragon Omelette, Honeydew Melon and Grapefruit Juice. *Above:* Baby Camemberts.

FRESH STRAWBERRIES WITH FROMAGE BLANC

Fromage blanc is a soft, fresh, unripened curd cheese made from either sheep's, goat's or cow's milk. It is delicious served with fresh berries in season and sprinkled with a little caster (superfine) sugar. It is also good beaten and mixed with crème fraîche and sprinkled with sugar.

Serve with buttermilk for a soothing, wholesome start to the day.

BABY CAMEMBERTS

Baby camemberts ('Berties') (pictured above) served with crusty French bread make a nice addition to the breakfast table.

MENU

A Picnic in the Garden

*Plan this spring picnic for a farm or large garden so that
you can pick your own fresh salad greens,
ready to eat straight away.*

ARTICHOKES AND ASPARAGUS VINAIGRETTE

~

YABBIES (FRESHWATER CRAYFISH) WITH SAFFRON MAYONNAISE

~

POTATO SALAD

~

SALAD, FRESH-PICKED FROM THE GARDEN

~

RUM-SOAKED APRICOT SAVARIN

Serves 6–8

ARTICHOKES AND ASPARAGUS VINAIGRETTE

FRESH ARTICHOKES AND ASPARAGUS ARE AT THEIR PEAK IN
SPRING. THEY ARE BEST WHEN PREPARED SIMPLY AND SERVED WITH
A HOME-MADE MAYONNAISE OR VINAIGRETTE DRESSING.

THE ASPARAGUS

Allow about 8 spears per person

Wash the asparagus and cut off their woody ends. Make sure they are all the same length. Cook them in rapidly boiling salted water for 5–8 minutes (the time will depend on their thickness). Alternatively, you can steam them.

Remove from heat and run under cold water to refresh.

Serve with mayonnaise or drizzled with dressing.

THE ARTICHOKES

Allow 1 medium globe artichoke per person

The artichokes will require more preparation than the asparagus. Have a bowl of acidulated water ready to plunge them into as they discolour once cut. To prepare the water, add the juice of half a lemon for every litre (1 quart) of water.

Wash the artichokes and trim the stems. Pull off any coarse outer leaves and cut any sharp tips with a pair of scissors. Put immediately into the bowl of water.

Bring a large non-aluminium pan of salted water to the boil, and cook the artichokes until they are tender (20–40 minutes). (If you cover the artichokes with a teatowel (dishcloth) they'll stay under water while cooking.) The time will depend on their size. You will know they are cooked when you can easily pull one of the leaves away. Remove with tongs from the water and turn upside down to drain. Let cool.

To serve, pull off a leaf and dip the base of the leaf into a vinaigrette or mayonnaise. Scrape away the lovely soft flesh with your teeth, discarding the rest of the leaf.

Previous page: Yabbies (Freshwater Crayfish), Artichoke and Asparagus Vinaigrette, and, in the background, Potato Salad.
Below: Artichokes and Asparagus Vinaigrette.
Right: Yabbies (Freshwater Crayfish).

YABBIES (FRESHWATER CRAYFISH) WITH SAFFRON MAYONNAISE

PREPARE THE YABBIES THE DAY BEFORE. IT IS BEST TO USE LIVE YABBIES. PUT THEM IN THE FREEZER BEFORE PLUNGING IN THE BOILING WATER. YOU CAN SUBSTITUTE LARGE SHRIMPS FOR THE CRAYFISH.

INGREDIENTS

1.5–2 kg (3 – 4 lb) live yabbies (freshwater crayfish)
~
10 cups (2.5 L, 2½ qt) water
~
60 g (2 oz) salt
~
1 tablespoon white granulated sugar
~
1 small can (375 ml, 13 fl oz) beer (optional)
~
3 tablespoons dill seed
~
1 bunch fresh dill

Heat water, salt, sugar, beer and dill in a large pot. Bring to a rolling boil. Add the yabbies 6 to 8 at a time, starting with the largest, bringing water back to the boil each time. Cook 8–10 minutes and remove with tongs or a large slotted spoon and put in a bowl with the fresh dill. Reserve the liquid.

Strain the cooking liquid over the yabbies and cool. When cold, put them in the refrigerator overnight, covered.

Remove the yabbies from the refrigerator, put on a platter, pour over a little of the cooking liquid and serve with the saffron mayonnaise and fresh crusty bread.

SAFFRON MAYONNAISE

INGREDIENTS

good pinch saffron threads, soaked in 1 tablespoon white wine vinegar for an hour

~

1½ teaspoons dried mustard powder

~

½ teaspoon salt

~

pinch white pepper

~

3 large fresh egg yolks, at room temperature

~

1½ – 1¾ cups (350–400 ml, 12–13 ½ fl oz) olive oil

Make sure all ingredients are at room temperature. Put the saffron vinegar, mustard powder, salt, pepper and egg yolks into the food processor bowl. Process to combine. With the motor still running, add the oil very slowly in drops from a teaspoon. As the mixture thickens, increase the flow of oil so that it becomes a thin steady stream. Stop pouring occasionally to check it has been well incorporated. When all the oil has been added, turn off and taste for seasoning. Add a little more vinegar or lemon juice, to taste, and if it seems too heavy, add 1–2 tablespoons of hot water before using.

POTATO SALAD

INGREDIENTS

1.5 kg (3 lb) medium-sized potatoes, unpeeled, washed and scrubbed

~

olive oil

~

flaky sea salt

~

white wine vinegar (optional)

~

pinch cayenne

~

dill

Steam or simmer the potatoes until just cooked. While still hot, cut them in quarters.

Put them into a salad bowl and sprinkle with olive oil, crushed sea salt, vinegar and cayenne. Toss well while hot and leave to cool.

Garnish with the freshly chopped dill.

SALAD OF YOUNG SPRING GREENS

Pick fresh young greens from the garden — cos (romaine) lettuce, red and green oakleaf (feuille de Chène, red salad bowl) mizuna (a small cut-leaf mustard green), French sorrel, baby silverbeet (Swiss chard) and rainbow chard, rocket (arugula), Lebanese (salad) cress, chervil and borage flowers. Toss together lightly and drizzle with good-quality olive oil and a little red or white wine vinegar. Season to taste.

Right: Fresh asparagus is a wonderful spring vegetable.

RUM-SOAKED APRICOT SAVARIN

THIS CAKE MUST BE BAKED IN A SAVARIN MOULD — THIS IS A RING MOULD
WITH CURVED SIDES.

INGREDIENTS

DOUGH
2 cups (250 g, 8 oz) plain (all-purpose) flour
~
¼ teaspoon salt
~
2 teaspoons (1 sachet, packet) dry (baker's) yeast
~
1 tablespoon white granulated sugar
~
1 cup (250 ml, 8 fl oz) warm (blood temperature) milk
~
3 eggs
~
200 g (7 oz) unsalted (sweet) butter, softened
~
250 g (8 oz) dried apricots, soaked overnight in the sugar syrup
~
(single, light) cream, for decoration

SYRUP
1 cup (250 g, 8 oz) white granulated sugar
~
1 cup (250 ml, 8 fl oz) water
~
½ vanilla bean, split
~
rind of ½ orange
~
100 ml (3½ fl oz) dark rum

Sift the flour and salt into a large bowl. In another smaller bowl, put the yeast, sugar and 2 tablespoons of the warm milk. Stir well and let stand 10 minutes. Make a well in the centre of the flour and pour in the yeast mixture. Add the remaining warm milk and stir well to combine. Beat the eggs well and add to the dough, beating thoroughly to combine. Put the mixture into a lightly oiled bowl and cover with a floured teatowel (dishcloth). Leave to stand in a warm place for 1 hour or until doubled in bulk.

Punch down the dough and vigorously stir in the softened butter, a small amount at a time, until well incorporated. Beat well until the dough is smooth and elastic. Butter and flour a 23 cm (9 in) savarin tin. Pour in the dough and cover with the cloth. Leave to stand until mixture has reached the top of the tin (about 45 minutes). Preheat oven to 200°C (400°F) and bake savarin for 20 minutes. Remove from the oven, turn out onto a cake rack. Put a plate underneath and ladle over the syrup while the savarin is hot. Fill the centre of the cake with the soaked apricots, decorate with freshly whipped cream and drizzle with the remaining syrup.

SYRUP

Combine all ingredients, except the rum, and bring to the boil, stirring well until sugar dissolves. Simmer gently for 15 minutes until syrupy. Pour in the rum and bring back to the boil. Remove from heat. Take out the vanilla pod and orange peel.

A day so happy.
Fog lifted early, I worked in the garden.
Hummingbirds were stopping over honeysuckle flowers.
There was no thing on earth I wanted to possess.
I knew no one worth my envying him.
Whatever evil I had suffered, I forgot.
To think that once I was the same man did not embarrass me.
In my body I felt no pain.
When straightening up, I saw the blue sea and sails.

CZESLAW MILOSZ, *GIFT*

Left: Rum-soaked Apricot Savarin.

MENU

An Afternoon Tea

A celebration of roses in bloom.

BLOWAWAY SPONGE

~

CRYSTALLISED ROSE PETALS

~

ROSE PETAL JAM

~

TURKISH DELIGHT

~

PYRAMID OF BERRIES WITH FRESH CREAM OR MASCARPONE

~

ROSE PETAL HEART-SHAPED BISCUITS (COOKIES)

Serves 8–10

BLOWAWAY SPONGE

A VERY LIGHT SPONGE WHICH SHOULD BE EATEN ON THE DAY YOU MAKE IT. USE VERY FRESH EGGS AT ROOM TEMPERATURE FOR BEST RESULTS.

INGREDIENTS

4 eggs, separated

~

pinch of salt

~

½ cup (110 g, 4 oz) caster (superfine) sugar

~

½ cup (65 g, 2 oz) cornflour (US cornstarch)

~

2 teaspoons plain (all-purpose) flour

~

1 teaspoon cream of tartar

~

½ teaspoon bicarbonate of soda (baking soda)

~

icing (powdered) sugar for dusting

~

(single, light) cream for filling

~

rose petal jam (see recipe page 36) for decoration

Grease and flour two 20 cm (8 in) sandwich tins (layer cake pans). Preheat oven to 190°C (375°F).

Beat the egg whites with a pinch of salt until stiff, then gradually add the sugar until thick and glossy. While still beating, add the yolks one at a time and continue beating until mixture forms a ribbon on top. Sift the remaining ingredients and fold gently through the egg mixture.

Cook 20 minutes or until the tops spring back when touched with a finger and the cake has shrunk slightly away from the sides of the tin. Turn out immediately onto greaseproof (waxed) paper which has been dusted with icing (powdered) sugar.

When cool, fill with the whipped cream and rose petal jam.

CRYSTALLISED ROSE PETALS

INGREDIENTS

100 g (3½ oz) rose petals (approximately 10–15 roses)

~

1 egg white

~

pinch salt

~

water

~

approximately 1 cup (220 g, 8 oz) vanilla-flavoured caster (superfine) sugar

Wash the rose petals carefully, then pat dry or leave to drain on absorbent paper towels. Beat the egg white with the salt and 1 teaspoon of water until foamy. Brush gently onto each petal with a pastry brush. Make sure there is no excess egg white on the petal surfaces. You may require another egg white.

Shake or dust the sugar onto both sides of the petals so that they are delicately but evenly coated. Put on a tray lined with greaseproof (waxed) paper and allow to dry for 2–3 days. Store in an airtight container in the refrigerator until required.

Spring has returned. The earth is like a child that knows poems.

RAINER MARIA RILKE, *SONNETS TO ORPHEUS*

Previous page: Rose Petal Jam, Turkish Delight and Fresh Berries.
Right: Blowaway Sponge with Crystallised Rose Petals.

ROSE PETAL JAM

INGREDIENTS

200–225 g (7½ oz) rose petals, approximately 25 dark red roses

~

3 cups (750 ml, 25 fl oz) water

~

1½ cups (375 g, 13½ oz) white granulated sugar

~

2 tablespoons lemon juice

~

commercial pectin*

Heel* and wash the petals, then put into a large saucepan with the water. Bring to a boil, cover and simmer for 30 minutes. Strain, reserving liquid and petals.

Put the reserved liquid back in the pan, add the sugar and stir over medium heat until all the sugar is dissolved. Bring to a boil, add the lemon juice and commercial pectin and cook for 10 minutes or until the jam has reached setting point.

Remove from heat, stir in the reserved petals and pour into hot sterile jars. Seal when cold.

*NOTE: To heel a rose, remove the white part at the base of the petal.

To know how much commercial pectin to add, read the instructions on the side of the packet, as the quantity required varies according to the brand you use.

Makes about 2 cups (500 ml, 17 fl oz)

TURKISH DELIGHT

INGREDIENTS

4 tablespoons (50 g, 1½ oz) gelatine

~

2½ cups (625 ml, 21 fl oz) water

~

3¾ cups (900 g, 2 lb) white granulated sugar

~

1 strip orange peel

~

1 tablespoon (20 ml) rosewater

~

few drops cochineal (red food colouring)

~

1 cup (125 g, 4 oz) fresh pistachio nuts or roasted almonds, chopped

~

icing (powdered) sugar, sifted, mixed with a little cornflour (US cornstarch)

In a small saucepan, dissolve the gelatine in half the water over moderate heat. It should look clear and runny. In another heavy saucepan, dissolve the sugar in the remaining water with the strip of orange peel, stirring with a wooden spoon until dissolved. If crystals form on the side of the pan, brush down with a brush dipped in warm water. Bring to the boil, remove from heat and add the gelatine. Return to heat and simmer gently over low heat for 15–20 minutes, stirring all the time. Remove from heat, take out the orange peel and stir in the rosewater, cochineal and nuts. Cover the pan and leave for 15 minutes.

Skim off any skin that has formed on top and pour into a lamington tray (jelly roll pan) (28 cm x 18 cm x 3 cm (11 in x 7 in x 2¼ in)) which has been rinsed out with water. Allow to set, preferably overnight, in the refrigerator.

Sift together the icing sugar and cornflour and rub a little of this over the surface of the Turkish Delight. Using a sharp knife dipped in the icing sugar mixture, cut the Turkish Delight into squares and toss in the mixture. Decorate with edible silver paper (available from Indian or Middle Eastern food stores). Store between sheets of wax paper with more sifted icing sugar and cornflour placed between each sheet.

Right: Turkish Delight.

ROSE PETAL HEART-SHAPED BISCUITS (COOKIES)

~

INGREDIENTS

250 g (8 oz) unsalted butter, softened

~

⅔ cup (150 g, 5 oz) caster (superfine) sugar

~

1 egg

~

2½ cups (325 g, 11½ oz) plain (all-purpose) flour

~

pinch salt

~

1 fragrant red rose, washed and finely shredded

~

icing (powdered) sugar for dusting

Cream together the butter and sugar, beat in the egg. Sift together the flour and salt and fold into the butter mixture with the shredded rose petal. Wrap the dough in greaseproof (waxed) paper and chill in the refrigerator 1–2 hours.

Preheat oven to 180°C (350°F).

Roll out the dough to 3 mm (⅛ in) in thickness, and cut with heart-shaped cutters. If it seems brittle, soften by kneading gently with a little extra flour. Bake on greased baking trays (sheets) for 12–15 minutes or until lightly coloured. Remove and let cool on a cake rack. Dust with icing sugar.

Makes 45–50

PYRAMID OF BERRIES WITH FRESH CREAM OR MASCARPONE

Fresh berries in season, like mulberries, youngberries and blackberries, look wonderful piled in a pyramid on a glass stand. Served like this, free of any fussing, they are also at their best. All you need is some whipped cream or mascarpone (that delectable Italian soft cream cheese) to accompany them.

Above: Pyramid of Berries.
Right: Rose Petal Heart-shaped Biscuits (Cookies).

MENU

A Mediterranean Dinner

This dinner has a definite Mediterranean flavour, featuring seafood, olives and tomatoes.

BRAISED OCTOPUS IN RED WINE WITH CHAR-GRILLED OLIVE BREAD

~

RISOTTO PRIMAVERA

~

LEMON AND LIME TART

~

TINY AMARETTI

Serves 6–8

BRAISED OCTOPUS IN RED WINE

THE LEMONS ARE PRESERVED IN SALT, MOROCCAN-STYLE. THEY ARE AVAILABLE FROM SPECIALITY DELICATESSENS. YOU CAN SUBSTITUTE ORDINARY LEMONS.

INGREDIENTS

600 g (20 oz) medium-sized octopus

~

150 g (5 oz) kalamata olives

~

rind of 2 preserved lemons, cut in julienne strips

~

3 ripe tomatoes, finely diced

~

1 large red (Spanish) onion, sliced finely

~

2–3 garlic cloves, chopped finely

~

3 stalks basil, leaves only

~

4 stalks Continental (flat-leaf or Italian) parsley, leaves only

~

3 stalks fresh oregano, leaves only

~

1¼ cups (300 ml, 10 fl oz) red wine

~

150 ml (5 fl oz) olive oil

~

freshly ground black pepper

Cut octopus into eating-size portions: cut tentacles below the beak and slice into rounds. Remove head and cut into a butterfly-shape, removing the sac and innards. Wash well. Combine with remaining ingredients and marinate overnight.

Preheat oven to 180°C (350°F). Remove octopus from the refrigerator and cover with aluminium foil. Braise in oven for 1½ hours or until tender.

When cool, serve with char-grilled olive bread, more fresh basil leaves and halved cherry tomatoes.

NOTE: Purple-black kalamata olives are marinated in wine vinegar, and are generally slit, allowing the marinade to be absorbed by the flesh.

Previous page: Braised Octopus in Red Wine with Char-grilled Olive Bread; in the background, Risotto Primavera.

OLIVE BREAD

THIS BREAD ACCOMPANIES THE OCTOPUS. SLICE IT, BRUSH LIGHTLY WITH OLIVE OIL, THEN PAN-FRY OR CHAR-GRILL ON BOTH SIDES.

INGREDIENTS

2½ cups (625 ml, 20 fl oz) water, at blood temperature

~

14 g (½ oz) fresh yeast

~

1 tablespoon honey

~

840 g (1¾ lb) unbleached plain (all-purpose) flour

~

3 teaspoons salt

~

dash of olive oil

~

500 g (1 lb) black olives, pitted, preferably kalamata

In a large mixing bowl, combine water, yeast and honey, stirring well. Add flour, salt and olive oil and knead for 15–20 minutes, using a dough hook. The long kneading time helps develop the gluten in the flour, giving a good, coarse texture.

Work in the olives. Rest the dough in a clean, lightly oiled bowl in a warm place, covered with plastic (cling) wrap and a cloth. Let prove (rise) for 1 hour.

Preheat oven to 220°C (425°F).

Knock back (punch down) the dough and shape into a tight ball. Put the dough onto a lightly oiled baking tray (sheet), cover again and allow to rise until doubled in bulk. Slash the top of the dough and sprinkle with flour.

Bake in the oven for 1 hour. Remove and cool.

RISOTTO PRIMAVERA

INGREDIENTS

6–8 cups (1.5–2 L, 1½–2 qt) chicken stock

~

250 g (8 oz) asparagus, trimmed of woody ends and cut in 2 cm (¾ in) lengths

~

400 g (14 oz) young peas in their pods, shelled

~

40 ml (1½ fl oz) oil

~

60 g (2 oz) unsalted butter

~

250 g (8 oz) button mushrooms, sliced finely

~

1 medium onion, finely chopped

~

1 clove garlic, crushed

~

1⅔ cups (350 g, 12 oz) arborio (short-grain) rice

~

⅓ cup (45 g, 1½ oz) parmesan cheese, freshly grated

~

6 sun-dried tomatoes, sliced thinly

~

salt and pepper

~

extra parmesan for shavings

Bring the chicken stock to boiling point. Throw in the asparagus pieces and peas and cook 2–3 minutes. Strain, returning the stock to the saucepan and reserving the vegetables. Bring stock back to simmering point.

Heat the oil in a large frying pan (skillet). Add half the butter and when melted, sauté the mushrooms. When soft, remove with a slotted spoon and reserve.

Add remaining butter, onion and garlic to the pan and stir until softened. Add the rice. Keep stirring over low heat until all the grains are coated with the butter and oil. Turn up the heat and add the stock 150 ml (5 fl oz) at a time, stirring frequently, to ensure rice absorbs stock each time — this will take 20–25 minutes. The rice should be soft, creamy and 'al dente'. Fold through the asparagus pieces, the peas and the mushrooms. Stir in the parmesan cheese and sun-dried tomatoes and season to taste.

Remove from heat and serve immediately, garnished with shavings of fresh parmesan.

Below: Risotto Primavera.

LEMON AND LIME TART

START MAKING THIS LUSCIOUS TART THE DAY BEFORE SERVING.

INGREDIENTS

PASTRY

2 cups (250 g, 8 oz) plain (all-purpose) flour

~

⅔ cup (110 g, 3 ½ oz) icing (powdered) sugar

~

125 g (4 oz) unsalted butter, chopped in pieces

~

1 egg

~

1 egg white

FILLING

4 eggs

~

⅓ cup (75 g, 2½ oz) caster (superfine) sugar

~

150 ml (5 fl oz) thickened (double, heavy) cream

~

150 ml (5 fl oz) lemon or lime juice (or half and half), freshly squeezed

~

zest of 1 lemon or 2 limes

~

GARNISH

2 lemons

~

2 limes

~

⅔ cup (200 ml, 7 fl oz) water

~

2 tablespoons (40 ml) lime or lemon juice

~

½ cup (125 g, 4 oz) white granulated sugar

icing (powdered) sugar for dusting

Put the flour and icing sugar into a food processor and process for 30 seconds to combine. Add the butter and process until mixture forms into breadcrumbs. Add the egg and continue mixing. When dough wraps around the blades, remove from the bowl and knead lightly on a floured bench to combine thoroughly. Wrap in plastic (cling) wrap and refrigerate overnight.

Roll out the dough on a lightly floured board and line a 25–26 cm (10 in) loose-bottomed flan tin (quiche pan). Press the dough in firmly and trim any excess. Allow to rest in the refrigerator at least 1 hour.

Preheat oven to 200°C (400°F). Remove the pastry from the refrigerator and brush with a beaten egg white. Return to the refrigerator for 15 minutes, then bake until lightly coloured. Turn oven down to 150°C (300°F). Pour the filling into the prepared flan case (it is easier to do this if the shell remains on a rack in the oven so that you can fill it as high as possible without having to move it). Cook 30–35 minutes. It may look wobbly, but don't worry, as it will set as it cools. When cool, dust with icing sugar, garnish with lemon and lime slices and glaze with the syrup.

FILLING

Beat together the eggs and sugar until pale, mix in the cream, then add the juice and zest at the last minute.

GARNISH

Wash the lemons and limes well and slice thinly. Put the water, lemon juice and sugar into a saucepan, bring to the boil and simmer until the sugar is dissolved. Place the lemon and lime slices in the syrup and cook 15 minutes or until peel is glazed and tender. Remove carefully from the syrup and when cool enough to handle, decorate the top of the flan with the fruit.

NOTE: You can freeze the remaining pastry for further use, or make little biscuits (cookies) to serve as 'petits fours' with coffee. Roll out thinly and stamp with a tiny biscuit cutter. Place the dough on greased baking trays (sheets) and bake in an oven set at 180°C (350°F) 8–10 minutes or until a pale biscuit colour. Remove and cool. Dust with icing (powdered) sugar before serving.

Right: Lemon and Lime Tart.

TINY AMARETTI

SERVE THESE AS 'PETITS FOURS' WITH COFFEE. USING UNBLANCHED ALMONDS GIVES
A LOVELY NUTTY CONSISTENCY.

INGREDIENTS

1 ½ cups (250 g, 8 oz) unblanched almonds

~

1 cup (150 g, 5 oz) icing (powdered) sugar

~

2 egg whites

~

½ teaspoon cream of tartar

Toast the almonds in an oven set at 180°C (350°F) for 10–15 minutes, watching them carefully. Remove, let cool, then grind in the food processor until fairly fine.

Sift the icing sugar into a bowl. Stir through the almonds. In another bowl, whisk the egg whites and cream of tartar until stiff. Fold through the almond mixture.

Preheat oven to 180°C (350°F).

Drop teaspoonfuls of the mixture onto a baking tray (sheet) lined with non-stick baking paper. Place in the oven and cook at 180°C (350°F) for 2 minutes, then turn down to 100°C (200°F) and dry out for another hour. Remove and cool on a cake rack.

Makes 20–24

Left: Tiny Amaretti.
Below: Lemons and limes are marvellous fruits, in season for much of the year.

SUMMER

MENU

Early Morning at the Beach

*What could be nicer than this light, summery breakfast;
perfect at the beach.*

CORNMEAL (MAIZEMEAL) PANCAKES

~

POTATO, EGGPLANT (AUBERGINE) AND LEEK FRITTATA

~

PAN-FRIED SARDINES

~

HOME-MADE YOGHURT

Serves 6–8

CORNMEAL (MAIZEMEAL) PANCAKES

GOOD WITH HOME-MADE YOGHURT, HONEY OR MAPLE SYRUP.

INGREDIENTS

1 cup (165 g, 5½ oz) yellow cornmeal (maizemeal)

~

1 teaspoon salt

~

1 tablespoon maple syrup

~

1 cup (250 ml, 8 fl oz) boiling water

~

2 eggs

~

½ cup (125 ml, 4 fl oz) milk

~

30 g (1 oz) butter, melted

~

½ cup (60 g, 2 oz) plain (all-purpose) flour

~

2 teaspoons baking powder

Put the cornmeal, salt and syrup into a bowl and pour over the boiling water. Stir to combine. Let stand 10 minutes.

In another bowl, beat together the eggs, milk and melted butter and stir into the softened cornmeal. Sift together the flour and baking powder and stir into the cornmeal mixture. Cook on a lightly greased hot plate or heavy frying pan (skillet). When bubbles appear, turn the pancake over and cook until golden on the other side. Repeat with the remaining mixture.

Makes 12

POTATO, EGGPLANT (AUBERGINE) AND LEEK FRITTATA

INGREDIENTS

2 medium potatoes (about 400 g, 14 oz), peeled and thinly sliced

~

⅓ cup (90 ml, 3 fl oz) olive oil

~

200 g (7 oz) eggplant (aubergine), peeled and thinly sliced

~

1 medium leek, washed and sliced in half lengthwise

~

salt and pepper

~

6 eggs

~

½ cup (60 g, 2 oz) parmesan cheese, freshly grated

~

½ bunch fresh basil, chopped

~

3 teaspoons (15 g, ½ oz) butter

Drop the potatoes into boiling salted water and cook 5–7 minutes, or until just becoming soft. Drain well.

Heat the oil in a heavy oven-proof frying pan (skillet), add the eggplant and leek and sauté over medium heat until softened. Add the potatoes and season to taste.

Whisk the eggs until yolks and whites are combined. Stir in the vegetable mixture, parmesan cheese and basil.

Melt the butter in the pan. Pour in the egg mixture and cook over low heat for 15 minutes or until the eggs have begun to set and only the top remains runny. Heat the grill and put the frittata underneath to set the top. Remove from heat and slide onto a dish using a spatula.

Serve warm or cold, cut into pie-like wedges.

Previous page: In the foreground, Potato, Eggplant (Aubergine) and Leek Frittata; left, Cornmeal (Maizemeal) Pancakes and Home-made Yoghurt; centre, Pan-fried Sardines. A variety of cheeses — creme de la creme, cheddar and parmigiano reggiano — and fresh bread, complete this picnic breakfast.
Right: Potato, Eggplant (Aubergine) and Leek Frittata.

PAN-FRIED SARDINES

INGREDIENTS

Allow 3–4 sardines per person

~

oil

~

flour

~

lemon wedges

Gently pull out the insides of each sardine. The backbone can be left in as it is soft enough to eat. Wash well and pat dry with paper towels (absorbent kitchen paper). Dust with a little flour. Heat some oil in a frying pan (skillet) or lightly oil a cast-iron ridged pan and fry the sardines on both sides until cooked. Cook in several batches. Serve with wedges of lemon.

HOME-MADE YOGHURT

INGREDIENTS

4 cups (1 L, 1 qt) milk

~

4 tablespoons (80 ml, 3 fl oz) natural (plain) yoghurt

Put the milk into a saucepan and bring to the boil. When it begins to froth, remove from heat and pour into a casserole dish. If you want a thicker yoghurt, evaporate some of the water from the milk by letting it simmer 20 minutes over low heat.

Leave until milk is warm (45°C, 115°F). Skim off the film from top of milk and mix in the yoghurt, stirring only a few times to blend. Cover with a lid, wrap in a thick cloth and leave undisturbed in a warm place for 8–10 hours or until thickened. Chill for at least 4 hours before using.

Makes about 3 cups (750 ml, 25½ fl oz)

...And still ahead : summer.
Not only all the dawns of summer —, not only
how they change themselves into day
and shine with beginning.
Not only the days, so tender around flowers and, above,
around the patterned treetops, so strong, so intense.
Not only the reverence of all these unfolded powers,
not only the pathways, not only the meadows at sunset,
not only, after a late storm, the deep-breathing freshness,
not only the approaching sleep, and a premonition...
but also the nights! But also the lofty summer
nights, and the stars as well, the stars of the earth.
Oh to be dead at last and know them endlessly,
all the stars: for how, how could we ever forget them!

RILKE, *THE SEVENTH ELEGY*

Right: Pan-fried Sardines.

MENU

Lunch outside the Beach House

*This menu is ideal for outdoor entertaining as most of the recipes
can be prepared ahead and assembled at the last minute.*

CEVICHE

~

BARBECUED QUAIL MARINATED IN OIL AND THYME

~

BRUSCHETTA WITH SUN-DRIED TOMATO PASTE

~

FENNEL AND ROCKET (ARUGULA) SALAD

~

FRESH MANGOES WITH MANGO GRANITA

~

OLD-FASHIONED POUND CAKE

Serves 6

CEVICHE

THE FISH IS POACHED IN LEMON AND LIME JUICE IN THIS LOVELY,
REFRESHING SALAD.

INGREDIENTS

*750 g (1½ lb) firm-fleshed fish fillets, such as salmon and
bream*

~

¼ cup (60 ml, 2 fl oz) lemon juice, freshly squeezed

~

½ cup (125 ml, 4 fl oz) lime juice, freshly squeezed

~

4–6 shallots (spring onions, scallions), sliced on the diagonal

~

1 stalk fresh lemon grass (takrai), sliced on the diagonal

~

1 Lebanese cucumber, thinly sliced

~

1–2 green chillies, finely chopped (optional)

~

500 g (1 lb) medium prawns (shrimps), cooked and peeled

~

2 cups (500 mls, 17 fl oz) coconut milk

~

salt, to taste

~

½ bunch fresh coriander (Chinese parsley), chopped

Remove skin and all the bones from the fish, using tweezers if
necessary. Slice into thin strips and put into an enamel or glass
bowl.

Cover the fish with the lemon and lime juices and leave for 2
hours, covered, in the refrigerator.

Remove and add remaining ingredients, stirring gently until
well combined. Serve immediately.

NOTE: Try to find a Lebanese cucumber for this recipe as the
skin is much softer than that of an ordinary cucumber, and
doesn't need to be removed.

Previous page: In the foreground, Bruschetta with Sun-dried Tomato Paste; left, Barbecued
Quail Marinated in Oil and Thyme; right, Fresh Mangoes; and, in the background, Old-
fashioned Pound Cake.
Right: Ceviche.

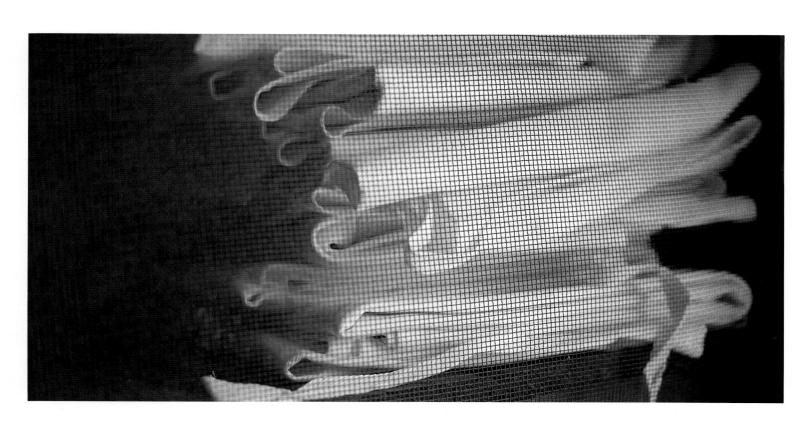

BARBECUED QUAIL MARINATED IN OIL AND THYME

INGREDIENTS

12 quail

~

1¼ cups (300 ml, 10 fl oz) olive oil

~

1 bunch fresh lemon thyme, leaves only

~

1 clove garlic, peeled and crushed

~

1 bay (laurel) leaf

~

10 parsley stalks

~

cracked black pepper

Snip wing tips from the quail, then cut down their backbones with a pair of kitchen scissors. Press down hard on the breast bones to flatten.

Place the quails in a large earthenware dish, pour over the oil and add the thyme, garlic, bay leaf, parsley and cracked pepper. Marinate, covered, for at least 3 hours, turning occasionally.

Light the barbecue and cook the quail on both sides for 4–5 minutes. Serve with Bruschetta.

Below: Barbecued Quail Marinated in Oil and Thyme with Fennel and Rocket (Arugula) Salad.

BRUSCHETTA WITH SUN-DRIED TOMATO PASTE

YOU CAN SUBSTITUTE PLAIN TOMATO PASTE IF YOU CAN'T FIND SUN-DRIED TOMATO PASTE.

INGREDIENTS

1 French bread stick (long, thin loaf)

~

olive oil

~

1 garlic clove, halved

~

sun-dried tomato paste

~

a few sun-dried tomatoes, cut in julienne strips

Cut the bread diagonally into medium-sized slices. Cook on the barbecue, watching carefully and turning when golden.

Brush with a little olive oil, rub with the garlic and smear with the paste.

Strew with the sun-dried tomato strips.

Above: Bruschetta with Sun-dried Tomato Paste.

FENNEL AND ROCKET (ARUGULA) SALAD

INGREDIENTS

1–2 fennel bulbs

~

1 bunch rocket (arugula)

~

approximately ½ cup (125 ml, 4 fl oz) vinaigrette dressing

~

½ red (Spanish) onion, thinly sliced

~

handful black olives

Slice the fennel and wash well. Remove leaves from the rocket and wash. Dry both the fennel and rocket.

Toss with the dressing, and strew with onion rings and black olives.

FRESH MANGOES WITH MANGO GRANITA

PEEL 4 MEDIUM-SIZED, FRESH RIPE MANGOES AND CUT INTO A PRETTY 'HEDGEHOG' PATTERN TO SERVE WITH THE GRANITA.

INGREDIENTS (GRANITA)

2 fresh ripe mangoes

~

⅓–½ cup (100 ml, 3½ fl oz) botrytis Rhine Riesling or Sauternes

~

juice and zest of 1 lime

~

water

~

1 tablespoon icing (powdered) sugar, sifted

Peel the mangoes and purée the flesh in a blender with the wine and lime juice and zest. Remove and measure the pulp, then stir in an equal quantity of water. Add the sugar. Stir well to combine, then pour into a 20 cm (8 in) square tray. Place the tray in the freezer. Remove the tray occasionally and give the mixture a good stir to help break up the crystals. When almost set, put the mixture in a food processor and purée. Return to the freezer until frozen solid.

Let the granita sit for 10–15 minutes outside the freezer to soften before serving. Serve with a wedge of lime and the fresh mangoes.

Summer afternoon — summer afternoon; to me those have always been the two most beautiful words in the English language.

HENRY JAMES

Right: Fresh Mangoes with Mango Granita.

OLD-FASHIONED POUND CAKE

~

INGREDIENTS

450 g (15 oz) unsalted (sweet) butter, softened

~

4 cups (500 g, 1 lb) plain (all-purpose) flour, sifted

~

10 eggs, separated

~

2 cups (500 g, 1 lb) white granulated sugar

~

1 teaspoon vanilla essence (extract)

Preheat oven to 165°C (325°F). Line a 23 cm (9 in) square tin with non-stick baking paper.

Cream the butter and work in the flour until the mixture is mealy. In a large bowl, beat the egg yolks with the sugar and vanilla until thick. Add the butter/flour mixture gradually. Fold in the stiffly beaten egg whites. Beat vigorously. Spoon into the prepared tin and bake 1½ hours. Remove and turn out on a cake rack. When cool, wrap in brown paper to take to the beach.

MENU

Dinner inside the Beach House

A menu inspired by the bounty of the sea.

CHILLI MUSSELS

~

ROCKPOOL'S TUNA IN HERB AND SPICE CRUST

~

BRAISED EGGPLANT (AUBERGINE)

~

RED CAPSICUM PURÉE

~

PEACHES POACHED IN THEIR OWN PINK SYRUP

Serves 6

CHILLI MUSSELS

INGREDIENTS

60 mussels (allow 10 per person)

~

vermouth

~

1½ tablespoons (30 ml, 1 fl oz) oil

~

2 cloves garlic, sliced

~

1–2 small red chillies, cut into julienne strips

~

6 ripe tomatoes, peeled and cut into dice

~

1 bunch coriander (Chinese parsley), leaves only

~

salt and pepper

Clean the mussels well: scrub the shells and remove the beard. Put a dash or two of vermouth in a large pan which has a tight-fitting lid. Throw in a quarter of the mussels, put on the lid and shake over high heat, removing the mussels as they open. Discard any which do not open. Repeat procedure until all the mussels are cooked.

Heat the oil in another pan, add the garlic and chilli and sauté until softened but not coloured. Add the tomatoes and stir until heated through. Add half the coriander, roughly chopped. Season to taste, then add the mussels along with all of their juices and shake or stir well to combine.

Spoon into soup bowls and garnish generously with the remaining coriander leaves.

ROCKPOOL'S TUNA IN HERB AND SPICE CRUST

ADAPTED FROM A RECIPE OF CHEF NEIL PERRY, WHO RUNS SYDNEY'S VERY SUCCESSFUL ROCKPOOL RESTAURANT.

INGREDIENTS

⅓ small bunch Continental (flat-leaf or Italian) parsley

~

⅓ small bunch fresh coriander (Chinese parsley)

~

1 red (Spanish) onion, peeled and chopped

~

2 garlic cloves, peeled

~

2 teaspoons each cumin powder, turmeric powder and chilli powder

~

1 teaspoon paprika

~

½ teaspoon salt

~

olive oil

~

2 teaspoons lemon juice

~

6 tuna steaks

Remove leaves from parsley and coriander and put into the blender or food processor with the onion, garlic, spices and salt with enough olive oil to make a thick paste. Stir in the lemon juice.

Coat the tuna steaks with the paste. Let sit ½ an hour, then sear in a very hot frying pan (skillet), preferably cast iron. Cook on one side until the paste is blackened and crusty. Turn and cook on the other side until the tuna is medium rare. Put a spoonful of Braised Eggplant (Aubergine) on a plate and top with Red Capsicum (Sweet Pepper) Purée. Place the tuna steak on top and finish with a squeeze of lemon juice.

Serve the tuna with couscous — use the precooked type tossed with a little melted butter or oil — and steamed snow peas (mangetout). Prepare the peas by stringing them and removing their top ends. Throw into a pot of rapidly boiling salted water for a minute, drain, and run under cold water.

Previous page: Centre, Rockpool's Tuna in Herb and Spice Crust with Braised Eggplant (Aubergine) and Red Capsicum (Sweet Pepper) Pureé; right, Chilli Mussels; and in the background, Couscous. *Right:* The capsicum is one of my favourite summer vegetables.

BRAISED EGGPLANT (AUBERGINE)

~

INGREDIENTS

2 medium eggplants (aubergines)

~

4 very ripe tomatoes

~

2 teaspoons cumin powder

~

approximately 1 cup (250 ml, 8 fl oz) olive oil

~

⅓ bunch Continental (flat-leaf or Italian) parsley, leaves only

~

lemon juice

~

salt and pepper

Wash the eggplants and slice into ½ cm (¼ in) rounds. Salt well and leave to drain in a colander for 1 hour. Skin the tomatoes by plunging into rapidly boiling water for 30 seconds. Remove with a slotted spoon to a bowl of cold water, then pull off skins. Chop the tomatoes and mix the cumin powder into the flesh.

Rinse and dry the eggplants on paper towels (absorbent kitchen paper). Heat the oil in a pan and fry the eggplant on both sides until golden. Quickly fry the parsley leaves until crisp but not brown. (The parsley leaves will splutter when they hit the oil, so be careful.) Leave a little of the oil in the pan, add the tomatoes and cook until soft. Return the eggplants and parsley to the tomatoes and mix well. Simmer the mixture gently for 30 minutes or until eggplants are tender. Cover with a lid, if necessary. Remove and add lemon juice, salt and pepper to taste.

RED CAPSICUM (SWEET PEPPER) PURÉE

~

INGREDIENTS

2 red capsicums (sweet peppers)

~

1 tablespoon (20 ml) virgin olive oil

~

few drops balsamic vinegar

~

salt and pepper

Heat the grill (broiler). Wash the capsicums, split in half and remove seeds. Place skin-side up under grill and cook until blackened and blistered. Put into a plastic bag to steam and when cool enough to handle, skin the capsicums. Purée the flesh in an electric blender or food processor. Remove from the blender and stir in the olive oil, balsamic vinegar and salt and pepper by hand, stirring well until smooth and a lovely glossy red colour.

We welcome summer and the glorious blessing of light.
We are rich with light; we are loved by the sun.
Let us empty our hearts into the brilliance.
Let us pour our darkness into the glorious, forgiving light.
For this loving abundance let us give thanks and offer our joy.
Amen

MICHAEL LEUNIG, *THE PRAYER TREE*

Left: The sensuous beauty of eggplants (aubergines).

PEACHES POACHED IN THEIR OWN PINK SYRUP

~

INGREDIENTS

4½ cups (1 kg, 2 lb 3 oz) caster (superfine) sugar

~

8 cups (2 L, 2 qt) water

~

1 vanilla bean

~

12 medium peaches

In a large pot, dissolve the sugar in the water and add the vanilla bean, bringing slowly to the boil. Turn down to simmer.

Drop in the peaches very carefully and cover them with a clean, wet teatowel (dishcloth) (this keeps them immersed in the syrup as they cook). Simmer very gently for 10 minutes.

Fill a large bowl three-quarters full with cold water. With a spoon, take out the peaches very carefully and plunge them in the water. Slip off the skins from bottom to top. Stand each peach alone so as not to damage the flesh. Meanwhile reduce the sugar syrup to a runny toffee consistency.

Put two perfect peaches into each dessert bowl and ladle over a little of the glorious pink syrup.

Above: Glorious summer peaches.
Right: Peaches Poached in their own Pink Syrup.

MENU

A Summer Buffet

An exotic menu which combines Asian flavours with fresh fruits and vegetables. It is topped off with a festive ice cream.

PARADISE SOUP

~

JELLIED CHICKEN WITH TOMATO CHILLI JAM

~

TERRINE DE CAMPAGNE

~

STEAMED ZUCCHINI (COURGETTE) FLOWERS

~

HONEYDEW MELON JUICE

~

MALAYSIAN SALAD

~

PLUM PUDDING ICE CREAM

Serves 6–8

PARADISE SOUP

THE TOMATOES NEED TO BE AT THEIR PEAK IN BOTH FLAVOUR AND COLOUR FOR
THIS SOUP TO WORK BEST.

INGREDIENTS

2 kg (4½ lb) very ripe tomatoes, peeled and chopped

~

2 small onions, minced

~

approximately 2 cups (500 ml, 16 fl oz) chicken stock

~

salt and pepper

~

½ honeydew melon

~

½ rockmelon (cantaloupe)

~

200 ml (7 fl oz) crème fraîche

~

fresh mint for garnishing (optional)

Put the tomatoes into the food processor and process until smooth. Remove and stir through the onions. Add enough chicken stock to make the mixture a soupy consistency. Add salt and pepper to taste and stir well to combine. Chill.

Remove the seeds from the melons and, with a melon baller, make balls out of the flesh. Place the balls in a bowl; cover and chill.

When ready to serve, ladle the chilled soup into bowls, put a dollop of crème fraîche on top and garnish with the melon balls and a little fresh mint if liked. Serve with lavash, the thin, crispy Middle Eastern bread.

JELLIED CHICKEN

ENGLISH CHEF RALPH POTTER MAKES THIS FOR GUESTS TO TAKE ON PICNICS WHEN
THEY STAY AT LILIANFELS GUESTHOUSE IN THE BLUE MOUNTAINS WEST OF SYDNEY.
THE TOMATO CHILLI JAM IS A NICE ACCOMPANIMENT.

INGREDIENTS

10–12 chicken thighs

~

approximately 8 cups (2 L, 2 qt) water

~

1 bay (laurel) leaf

~

peppercorns

~

1 onion

~

1 carrot

~

1 celery stalk

~

olive oil

~

3 teaspoons (10 g) gelatine (optional)

~

salt and pepper

~

small bunch each of fresh parsley, chervil and basil, chopped

Remove the flesh from the thighs and cut into chunks. Reserve the bones. Put the chicken into the refrigerator until the stock is ready. To make the stock, put the bones into a large pot, cover with water and add a bay leaf, some peppercorns, an onion, scraped carrot and celery stalk. Bring to the boil, skim well, and simmer for 1½ hours. Remove and strain.

Seal the chicken pieces in a little hot olive oil in a heavy pan. Drain the pieces on paper towels (absorbent kitchen paper), then put them into a pan, covered with the stock. Bring to the boil, turn down and simmer until cooked.

Remove the chicken pieces and, using tongs, place them in a preserving jar or china terrine.

Meanwhile reduce the stock until there is just enough to cover the chicken pieces, add the gelatine and salt and pepper to taste and pass through a sieve. Stir through the chopped herbs and pour over the chicken. Leave in the refrigerator overnight to set.

Previous page: In the foreground, Steamed Zucchini (Courgette) Flowers; left, Jellied Chicken; right, Malaysian Salad and Tomato Chilli Jam; and, in the background, Terrine de Campagne and Honeydew Melon Juice.
Right: Paradise Soup with Lavash.

NOTE: This recipe will work without the gelatine — using it gives a firmer consistency.

TOMATO CHILLI JAM

A BEAUTIFUL, GLOSSY RELISH WHICH REQUIRES A BIT OF WATCHING.

INGREDIENTS

approximately 1 kg (2 lb) tomatoes

~

approximately 2 cups (500 g, 1 lb) white granulated sugar

~

2 hot red chillies, chopped

~

2 tablespoons (50 ml) balsamic vinegar

Blanch the tomatoes in boiling water for 1 minute, remove and run under cold water. Slip off their skins, cut into halves and remove the seeds. Cut the halves into smaller pieces and weigh them. Add to the tomatoes exactly half their weight in sugar (eg 1 kg (2 lb) tomatoes = 500 g (1 lb) sugar).

Leave to macerate overnight with the sugar, chillies and vinegar.

Next day, place the mixture in a heavy-bottomed pan over a low heat and cook until thick and dark, stirring frequently to prevent sticking. This will take 1–2 hours.

When the jam has reached setting point, spoon into sterilised jars, seal and leave to cool. The relish will keep several months in the refrigerator.

To test for setting point: put a saucer in the freezer. When it is cold, put a little of the jam mixture onto it — if it wrinkles when you push it with your finger, it is set.

TERRINE DE CAMPAGNE

EASY TO MAKE AND KEEPS WELL. TRY OVERLAPPING STRIPS OF THINLY SLICED PROSCIUTTO ALONG THE BOTTOM AND SIDES OF THE MOULD — THIS MAKES FOR A RICHER TERRINE.

INGREDIENTS

approximately 10–15 fresh vine leaves

~

2–3 bay (laurel) leaves

~

125 g (4 oz) unsalted (sweet) butter

~

2 onions, finely chopped

~

2 cloves garlic, crushed

~

1 kg (2 lb) finely minced (ground) veal and pork

~

500 g (1 lb) finely minced (ground) pork fat

~

500 g (1 lb) chicken or duck livers, sinews removed and chopped

~

250 g (8 oz) ham, cut into small dice

~

½ cup (125 ml, 4 fl oz) Cognac

~

½ cup (125 ml, 4 fl oz) thickened (double, heavy) cream

~

3 eggs, lightly beaten

~

3 teaspoons salt

~

black pepper, freshly ground

~

½ teaspoon each allspice, mace, dried rosemary and thyme

~

⅛ teaspoon ground cloves

Preheat oven to 180°C (350°F).

Wash the vine leaves and blanch them quickly in hot water. Refresh under cold water. Lightly oil 1 large terrine or 2 smaller ones and lay the vine leaves along the bottom and sides — you'll need about 12 for the large terrine, more if using small ones. Put 1 or 2 bay leaves on the bottom of each terrine.

Melt the butter in a heavy frying pan (skillet), add the onion and garlic and cook until translucent. In a large bowl, combine the remaining ingredients and add the onion/garlic mixture, mixing together well. Spoon into the terrine dish (or dishes) smoothing the mixture so that it is flat on top.

Place in a bain-marie (or place in a roasting pan half filled with water) and cover tightly with aluminium foil. Put into the oven. If cooking just 1 large terrine, allow 2 ½ hours covered, and another ½ hour uncovered. For smaller terrines, allow 1 ¾ hours and another ½ hour uncovered. Remove from oven when cooked, let cool and re-cover with aluminium foil. Place a heavy weight on the top and put in the refrigerator overnight to set.

Next day, remove the weights and foil. Ease the terrine away from the sides of the dish with a knife or dip the whole terrine quickly in warm water and turn out.

O for a lodge in a garden of cucumbers!
O for an iceberg or two at control!
O for a vale that at midday the dew cumbers!
O for a pleasure trip up to the pole!
ROSSITER JOHNSON, *NINETY-NINE IN THE SHADE*

Left: Terrine de Campagne.

STEAMED ZUCCHINI (COURGETTE) FLOWERS

INGREDIENTS

18–24 zucchini (courgette) flowers with the baby zucchini attached to the end (allow 2–3 zucchini flowers per person)

~

18–24 thin slices smoked mozzarella cheese

~

olive oil

~

few drops balsamic vinegar

~

black pepper

Wash the zucchini flowers and place them in a steamer, preferably bamboo, over a pan of steaming water.

Steam for about 3 minutes. Don't overcook them as the flowers will start to wilt. Remove and run quickly under cold water and let cool.

Wrap each zucchini in thinly sliced smoked mozzarella cheese and drizzle with olive oil and a few drops of balsamic vinegar. Grind some black pepper over the top and serve as crudités.

You can also wrap the zucchini in thinly sliced prosciutto.

HONEYDEW MELON JUICE

Chilled honeydew melon makes a delicious sweet drink when passed through the juicer. Peel the melons, remove the seeds and chop into chunks. Push the chunks through the juicer and serve over ice blocks. An average honeydew melon (1.5 kg (3 lb)) will yield about 1 L (1 qt) of juice.

Above: Zucchinis (courgettes) are lovely lightly steamed or fried in butter.
Right: Steamed Zucchini (Courgette) Flowers.

MALAYSIAN SALAD

~

I CAME ACROSS THIS LOVELY SALAD AT THE PENANG PARK ROYAL HOTEL. THE COMBINATION OF COLOURS, TEXTURES AND FLAVOURS IS BOTH SURPRISING AND DELICIOUS.

INGREDIENTS

1 pineapple, peeled, and with the core removed

~

1 large red (Spanish) onion

~

2 Lebanese cucumbers, unpeeled or 1 telegraph cucumber, peeled

~

1 large red chilli

~

1 bunch fresh coriander (Chinese parsley)

~

vinegar, sugar and lemon or lime juice, to taste

Cut the pineapple flesh into bite-size wedges. Peel the onion and cut it into eighths. Wash the cucumbers and cut them lengthwise into quarters, then into triangular shapes. Slice the chilli finely. Remove leaves from coriander. Toss together with the vinegar, sugar and lemon or lime juice, to taste.

PLUM PUDDING ICE CREAM

~

INGREDIENTS

¾ cup (125 g, 4 oz) mixed glacé (candied) fruits (apricots, figs, pineapple), chopped

~

⅓ cup (75 g, 2½ oz) sultanas (golden raisins)

~

⅓ cup (75 g, 2½ oz) currants

~

⅓ cup (60 g, 2 oz) mixed (candied) peel

~

⅓ cup (60 g, 2 oz) glacé (candied) ginger, chopped

~

⅔ cup (150 ml, 5 fl oz) brandy or dark rum

~

1⅓ cups (150 g, 5 oz) roasted almonds, chopped

~

½ teaspoon each ground cinnamon, mixed spice and nutmeg

~

2 L (2 qt) best-quality vanilla ice cream, softened

Mix together all the fruits in a bowl and pour in the brandy or rum. Stir well, cover and let stand overnight.

Next day mix the nuts and spices through the fruit. Put the ice cream into a bowl and break it up gently, then fold through the fruit and nut mixture. Rinse out a 2–2.5 L (2–2½ qt) mould with water and spoon in the ice cream. Cover with aluminium foil, place in the freezer, and leave to set overnight.

When ready to serve, dip the mould into hot water, then invert onto a serving platter. Cover the mould with a teatowel (dishcloth) which has been dipped in hot water and give it a good shake if the ice cream won't come out.

Serve immediately with fresh soft summer fruits like cherries, blueberries, raspberries and strawberries.

Heat, ma'am! It was so dreadful here that I found there was nothing left for it but to take off my flesh and sit in my bones.

SYDNEY SMITH

Right: Plum Pudding Ice Cream.

AUTUMN

MENU

An Autumn Breakfast

A menu that glows with the golds, oranges and reds of the season. It features tamarillos, apricots and pawpaw (papaya).

POACHED TAMARILLOS WITH CREAMED RICOTTA

~

ORANGE BRIOCHE WITH APRICOT RAISIN PRESERVE

~

POACHED EGGS WITH SMOKED SALMON

~

GRANOLA

~

PAWPAW (PAPAYA) AND MUSCATELS

Serves 6–8

POACHED TAMARILLOS

TAMARILLOS (ALSO KNOWN AS TREE TOMATOES) ORIGINATED IN SOUTH AMERICA, AND ARE NOW GROWN WIDELY IN NEW ZEALAND. THE FLAVOUR IS TART — A CROSS BETWEEN A TOMATO AND A PASSIONFRUIT.

INGREDIENTS

12–16 tamarillos

~

4 cups (1 L, 1 qt) water

~

1 cup (250 g, 8 oz) white granulated sugar

Drop the tamarillos into a saucepan of boiling water; remove from heat immediately and place in a bowl of cold water using a slotted spoon. Slit the skins with a sharp knife and slip them off. If the skins remain difficult to remove, repeat the process.

Bring 1 litre of water to the boil with the sugar, making sure the sugar dissolves before the water boils. Boil 3–4 minutes, then add the skinned tamarillos to the pan and poach gently for 12–15 minutes. Remove from heat and let the tamarillos cool in the syrup.

Serve the tamarillos in bowls with a scoop of Creamed Ricotta. Drizzle with some of the syrup.

CREAMED RICOTTA

INGREDIENTS

150 g (5 oz) fresh ricotta

~

200 ml (7 fl oz) crème fraîche

~

1–2 tablespoons icing (powdered) sugar (optional)

Put the ricotta and crème fraîche into a bowl and beat until smooth. Add sugar to taste. Serve with the tamarillos.

No Spring, nor Summer Beauty
hath such grace,
As I have seen in one Autumnall face.

JOHN DONNE

Previous page: In the foreground, Muscatels; left, Poached Eggs with Smoked Salmon; far left, Granola; right, Orange Brioche; and in the background, Fresh Tamarillos and Pawpaw (Papaya).
Right: Poached Tamarillos.

ORANGE BRIOCHE

INGREDIENTS

100 g (3½ oz) unsalted (sweet) butter

~

⅔ cup (200 ml, 7 fl oz) milk

~

¼ cup (60 g, 2 oz) caster (superfine) sugar

~

40 g (1⅓ oz) fresh yeast

~

juice and zest of 3 oranges

~

4 cups (500 g, 1 lb) plain (all-purpose) flour

~

pinch salt

~

5 egg yolks

GLAZE

1 egg yolk

~

1 tablespoon (20 ml) milk

Preheat oven to 180°C (350°F). Lightly grease two 22 x 7 x 6 cm (8½ x 2¾ x 2½ in) baking tins (pans) or 20 small brioche moulds.

Dissolve the butter in the milk in a saucepan, lower heat to blood temperature, then add the sugar and yeast. Stir well to dissolve the sugar and yeast.

Put the orange juice into a small saucepan and reduce by half. Let cool.

Put the flour and salt into a mixing bowl, add the orange zest and mix to combine with a dough hook. Pour in the yeast mixture and orange juice and begin to beat, adding 1 egg yolk at a time until the mixture is smooth and silky. Let prove (rise) in a warm place, covered with a teatowel (dishcloth), 25–30 minutes. Knock back (punch down) the dough, then put into the moulds. Let prove again until mixture has doubled. Brush the glaze lightly over the top of the brioche and bake in the preheated oven 20–25 minutes.

GLAZE

Beat together the egg yolk and milk.

APRICOT RAISIN PRESERVE

INSPIRED BY A RECIPE OF ANTON MOSIMANN.

INGREDIENTS

1½ cups (250 g, 8 oz) dried apricots

~

3 cups (750 ml, 25 fl oz) water

~

juice of 2 oranges

~

1 cinnamon stick

~

1 vanilla pod, split

~

⅓ cup (60 g, 2 oz) raisins plumped overnight in 2 tablespoons (40 ml) whisky

~

water

Soak the apricots overnight in the water and orange juice. Put into a saucepan with the cinnamon and vanilla pod and cook until soft and pulpy — about 30 minutes.

Put the plumped raisins into a saucepan and just cover with water. Cook until most of the liquid is absorbed. Drain and let cool.

When the apricots are cool, remove the cinnamon stick and vanilla pod and put into an electric blender or food processor. Purée until smooth. Mix the apricot purée through the raisins, cool and place in a dish. Store, covered, in the refrigerator.

Right: Apricot Raisin Preserve with Toast and Muscatels.

POACHED EGGS WITH SMOKED SALMON

INGREDIENTS

¼ teaspoon vinegar or lemon juice

~

12 fresh eggs

~

6 slices fresh hot buttered toast

~

6 generous slices smoked salmon

~

freshly ground black pepper

Use very fresh eggs from the refrigerator as they will hold their shape better. Half fill a shallow saucepan with water and bring to simmering point. Add ¼ teaspoon white vinegar or lemon juice. Break each egg first into a cup and then slide gently into the water, which should be at a rolling boil to help coagulate the white and restrain the yolk. As the eggs go in, the temperature will drop, so bring the water back to the boil then lower to simmering point. Cook two eggs at a time. Cook 2–3 minutes or until soft but firm. Remove carefully with a slotted spoon or egg slice and drain well.

Place the eggs gently on to pieces of prepared toast and top each pair with a generous slice of smoked salmon. Grind some fresh black peppercorns over the top.

GRANOLA

THIS MIXTURE MAKES A LARGE QUANTITY, SERVING 20–25 PEOPLE. IT WILL KEEP WELL STORED IN AIR-TIGHT JARS.

INGREDIENTS

1½ cups (250 g, 8 oz) dried apricots

~

1½ cups (250 g, 8 oz) dates

~

1⅓ cups (100 g, 3½ oz) dried apple

~

1¼ cups (200 g, 7 oz) sultanas (golden raisins)

~

1¼ cups (200 g, 7 oz) raisins

~

1¼ cups (300 g, 10½ oz) soy flakes

~

1½ cups (300 g, 10½ oz) rolled barley

~

2 cups (200 g, 7 oz) wheat germ

~

1 cup (125 g, 4 oz) sunflower seeds

~

1 cup (125 g, 4 oz) pepitas (pumpkin seeds)

~

¾ cup (125 g, 4 oz) unblanched almonds

~

1 cup (250 ml, 8 fl oz) vegetable oil

~

2 cups (750 ml, 24 fl oz) honey

Chop the dried apricots, dates and apples into small pieces and toss them in a very large bowl together with the sultanas, raisins, soy flakes, barley, wheat germ, seeds and nuts.

In a saucepan, heat the oil and honey until the honey has thoroughly melted. Toss this while warm through the fruit-grain mixture and distribute evenly, using a large wooden spoon.

Heat the oven to 150°C (300°F). Spread the mixture out evenly over two large baking trays (sheets) and toast slowly until golden brown, watching carefully to make sure it doesn't become too dark.

Remove and let cool. Store in air-tight containers and serve with soy milk, buttermilk, milk, yoghurt or fruit juice.

PAWPAW (PAPAYA) AND MUSCATELS

Pawpaw and breakfast somehow go hand in hand. Choose evenly coloured, bright-yellow, undamaged fruit with a sweet perfume. Pawpaw can be stored at room temperature for a few days until soft to the touch — this indicates peak ripeness. Cut into slices and serve with a wedge of lemon or lime to enhance the flavour. Muscatels — large fragrant raisins from the muscatel grape — are available loose or in bunches and make an attractive addition to the breakfast table.

Left: Poached Eggs with Smoked Salmon.

MENU

A Morning Tea

This is a wickedly indulgent morning tea in the best English tradition.

FIG AND GINGER SCONES (BISCUITS)

~

SOUR CREAM RASPBERRY TEACAKE

~

GOLDEN SYRUP TART

~

SHREDDED COCONUT MACAROONS

~

PEAR AND POLENTA PIE

~

WALNUT CRESCENTS

Serves 10–12

FIG AND GINGER SCONES (BISCUITS)

~

INGREDIENTS

3 cups (375 g, 13½ oz) self-raising flour

~

pinch of salt

~

1½ teaspoons dry ground ginger

~

1 teaspoon orange zest, finely grated

~

60 g (2 oz) softened butter

~

1 cup (185 g, 6 oz) dried figs, thinly sliced

~

1 cup (250 ml, 8 oz) milk, soured with 2 teaspoons lemon juice

~

milk for glazing

Preheat oven to 230°C (450°F). Lightly grease a baking tray (sheet).

Sift the flour together with the salt and dry ginger. Rub through the orange zest and butter until the mixture resembles breadcrumbs. Stir through the dried figs, then add the milk to make a soft dough, adding a little more if necessary. Bundle it all up together and turn out onto a floured board. Pat out to 2.5 cm (1 in) in thickness (make them generous) and cut into 12 rounds with a floured cutter.

Set the scones close together on the prepared tray. Brush with milk. Bake in the preheated oven for 15–20 minutes or until golden on top. Cool on a wire rack.

Variations: Chopped dates can be substituted for the figs.

SOUR CREAM RASPBERRY TEACAKE

~

INGREDIENTS

250 g (8 oz) softened butter

~

1 cup (250 g, 8 oz) white granulated sugar

~

1 teaspoon lemon zest, finely grated

~

3 eggs

~

2 cups (250 g, 8 oz) plain (all-purpose) flour

~

1 cup (125 g, 4 oz) self-raising flour

~

1½ teaspoons bicarbonate of soda (baking soda)

~

1½ cups (375 ml, 13½ oz) (dairy) sour cream

RASPBERRY FILLING

300 g (10½ oz) fresh raspberries

~

⅓ cup (60 g, 2 oz) brown (soft, light brown) sugar

~

1 cup (100 g, 3½ oz) flaked almonds

~

2 teaspoons cinnamon

icing (powdered) sugar for dusting

~

(single, light) cream

Preheat oven to 180°C (350°F). Grease a 26 cm (10 in) bundt tin (a round tin with deep sides and a hollow centre tube).

Cream together the butter, sugar and lemon zest until light and fluffy. Add the eggs one at a time, then fold in the sifted dry ingredients alternately with the sour cream.

Spoon half the mixture into the tin. Strew the Raspberry Filling over the cake mixture, then spoon over remaining cake mixture.

Bake in the preheated oven 50–60 minutes or until a skewer inserted in the centre comes out clean. Cool on a wire rack. Dust with icing sugar. Serve with whipped cream and more fresh raspberries.

RASPBERRY FILLING

Combine the raspberries, brown sugar, flaked almonds and cinnamon in a small bowl and toss lightly together.

Previous page: Centre, Golden Syrup Tart; left, Fig and Ginger Scones (Biscuits); right, Pear and Polenta Pie.
Right: In the foreground, Sour Cream and Raspberry Teacake; above left; Coconut Macaroons; above right, Walnut Crescents.

GOLDEN SYRUP TART

~

YOU CAN ALSO USE TREACLE FOR THIS RECIPE, THOUGH IT IS SLIGHTLY MORE BITTER.

INGREDIENTS

PASTRY

1⅔ cups (200 g, 7 oz) plain (all-purpose) flour

~

¼ cup (45 g, 1½ oz) pure icing (powdered) sugar

~

¼ teaspoon baking powder

~

125 g (4 oz) frozen butter, cut in cubes

~

1 egg

~

2–3 teaspoons (10–15 ml, ½ oz) single (light) cream

~

*egg wash

GOLDEN SYRUP FILLING

1½ cups fresh breadcrumbs (about 5 slices bread, trimmed)

~

1 cup (375 ml, 12 fl oz) golden syrup (cane syrup, corn syrup) or treacle

~

30 g (1 oz) butter

~

1½ tablespoons (30 ml, 1 fl oz) (single, light) cream

~

juice and grated zest of ½ lemon

~

½ teaspoon ground nutmeg

Preheat oven to 200°C (400°F).

Put the flour, icing sugar and baking powder together into a food processor. Process for 30 seconds to combine, then add the butter all at once and process until mixture resembles breadcrumbs.

Whisk together the egg and cream and add to the flour mixture. Process until mixture forms a ball around the blades. Remove and turn onto a floured board or marble slab. With the palm of your hand, push down and away from you, smearing the pastry on the workbench. Do this three times, to ensure the pastry is homogeneous.

Roll out the pastry and roll up onto a rolling pin. Line a 23 cm (9 in) pie dish with the pastry, reserving the remainder to make leaves. Cut out leaves with a small sharp knife and press onto outer edge with a little egg wash, draping some leaves over the sides to add character.

Pour the Golden Syrup Filling into the prepared case and bake in the preheated oven 25–30 minutes, or until the filling is golden.

GOLDEN SYRUP FILLING

Make the breadcrumbs. Put the golden syrup, butter and cream together into a medium saucepan and heat gently until it is a runny consistency. Add the lemon juice, zest and nutmeg. Remove from heat, cool a little and stir in the breadcrumbs.

*NOTE: Make egg wash by whisking 1 egg together with a teaspoon of water. Brush over leaves lightly.

It was the sight of apple blossom
on the tree outside the kitchen window
that set me to begin a book
I didn't know then what I saw
or what it was I did
but hope was there full as buds

and now I eat the apples
and the book feeds me...

KATE LLEWELLYN, *APPLES* (excerpt)

Left: Golden Syrup Tart.

SHREDDED COCONUT MACAROONS

INGREDIENTS

3 cups (150 g, 5 oz) shredded (flaked) coconut

~

1 teaspoon baking powder

~

4 teaspoons cornflour (US cornstarch)

~

5 egg whites

~

1⅓ cups (300 g, 10½ oz) caster (superfine) sugar

~

1 teaspoon vanilla essence (extract)

Preheat oven to 120°C (250°F). Lightly grease baking trays (sheets) and dust lightly with cornflour — or use non-stick baking paper.

Put the coconut, baking powder and cornflour together into a bowl and toss well to combine.

Whisk the egg whites in a copper or glass bowl until soft peaks form. Add the sugar gradually, whisking well after each addition.

Add vanilla, then quickly fold in the coconut mixture. Be careful not to overmix.

Place in large spoonfuls onto prepared trays. Bake in the preheated oven 50–60 minutes or until dry and crisp. Turn off the oven and let cool in the oven for ½ hour. Store in air-tight tins when cool.

Variation: A nice addition is a dollop of jam in the centre of each macaroon.

Makes 24

PEAR AND POLENTA PIE

INGREDIENTS

1¾ cups (200 g, 7 oz) plain (all-purpose) flour

~

⅔ cup (100 g, 3 oz) coarse polenta (cornmeal)

~

⅔ cup (150 g, 5 oz) caster (superfine) sugar

~

pinch salt

~

150 g (5 oz) softened butter, cut in small pieces

~

3 egg yolks

FILLING

5 large pears, about 1 kg (2 lb 3 oz), peeled

~

⅓ cup (100 g, 3½ oz) white granulated sugar

~

75 g (2½ oz) butter

~

2 star anise

~

rind and juice of 1½ lemons

~

¼ cup (60 ml, 3 fl oz) rum or brandy

~

1 tablespoon plain (all-purpose) flour

Preheat oven to 180°C (350°F).

Combine the flour, polenta, sugar and salt on the workbench (countertop) and make a well in the centre. Add the butter and yolks and mix with your hands to make a firm pastry.

Press half the pastry into a 23 cm (9 in) loose-bottomed flan tin. Roll out the remaining pastry between two sheets of plastic (cling) wrap to make a top for the pie. Place in the refrigerator until ready to use.

Spoon the filling into the prepared pastry shell. Top with the remaining pastry and brush with beaten egg wash (see page 97). Cook 35–40 minutes or until golden.

FILLING

Slice the pears into eighths, and remove the cores. Set aside. Melt the sugar and butter in a heavy frying pan (skillet) and cook until it begins to caramelise. Add sliced pears and stir well to coat. Add the star anise, lemon juice and rind and rum or brandy. Cook over medium high heat until some of the juices are reduced. Remove a little of the syrup and stir in the flour until smooth. Return the flour mixture to the pan and cook until juices are absorbed, 1–2 minutes. Cool.

WALNUT CRESCENTS

INGREDIENTS

2 cups (250 g, 8 oz) plain (all-purpose) flour

~

⅓ cup (90 g, 3 oz) caster (superfine) sugar

~

250 g (8 oz) unsalted butter, cut in small pieces

~

1¼ cups (125 g, 4 oz) ground walnuts

~

2 egg yolks

~

icing (powdered) sugar for dusting

Preheat oven to 180°C (350°F). Grease baking trays (sheets).

Sift the flour and sugar together into a bowl. Rub through the butter. Stir in the walnuts and egg yolks and knead together lightly until it is a soft consistency. The mixture will be slightly sticky, but that's okay.

Take walnut-size pieces of the mixture and roll into crescent shapes. Place on the prepared trays and cook for about 15 minutes or until a pale golden colour. Remove from the trays with a spatula while warm and cool on racks. When cold, dust with icing sugar and store in airtight containers with a vanilla bean.

Makes 50

MENU

A Thai Lunch

This is a Thai-inspired, spicy menu, rich with the flavours of lime leaves and chillies. The blancmanger is a suitably soothing finale.

THAI HOT AND SOUR SOUP

~

CHICKEN AND PUMPKIN CURRY

~

STEAMED JASMINE RICE

~

BLANCMANGER WITH RASPBERRY COULIS

~

PLATTER OF FRESH TROPICAL FRUITS

Serves 8–10

THAI HOT AND SOUR SOUP

USE THE CHICKEN BONES, LEFT OVER FROM THE CHICKEN AND PUMPKIN CURRY, TO MAKE THE BROTH FOR THIS PUNGENT SOUP. IF YOU DON'T LIKE IT HOT, REDUCE THE QUANTITY AND REMOVE SEEDS FROM CHILLIES BEFORE ADDING.

INGREDIENTS

chicken bones, fat removed

~

10 cups (2.5 L, 2¼ qt) water

~

2 stalks lemon grass (white part only), cut on diagonal

~

2 garlic cloves, peeled and flattened

~

6 Kaffir lime leaves, washed and torn

~

2 large tomatoes, washed and cut in eighths

~

¼ cup (60 ml, 2 fl oz) Thai fish sauce (nam pla)

~

10 stalks fresh coriander (Chinese parsley) (including root) cut in 3 cm (1½ in) lengths

~

200 g (7 oz) fresh button or oyster mushrooms

~

4–6 red chillies, washed and chopped

~

1 teaspoon sugar

~

salt to taste

~

juice 1 lemon or lime

Put the chicken bones and water into a pot or wok. Bring to the boil, then simmer 20–25 minutes, removing any scum that comes to the surface.

Drain through a sieve, retaining broth. Put broth back into pot together with the lemon grass, garlic, Kaffir lime leaves and tomatoes. Bring back to the boil and simmer 5–10 minutes. Add remaining ingredients, simmering another 10 minutes. Taste to check if it is too hot, too sour, and for sugar and salt. When to your liking, remove coriander stalks and serve immediately.

NOTE: Prawns (shrimps) are a nice addition to this soup — throw in 10–12 peeled and de-veined green prawns (fresh shrimps) a minute or two before serving. Cook until prawns are just pink.

He that high growth on cedars did bestowe
Gave also lowly mushrumpes leave to growe.

ROBERT SOUTHWELL, *POEMS*

Previous page: Chicken and Pumpkin Curry.
Right: Thai Hot and Sour Soup.

CHICKEN AND PUMPKIN CURRY

THIS CURRY IS BEST MADE THE DAY BEFORE AS THE FLAVOUR DEVELOPS OVERNIGHT. CHOOSE A FIRM-TEXTURED PUMPKIN WITH A GOOD ORANGE COLOUR.

INGREDIENTS

1 tablespoon (20 ml) vegetable oil

~

2 x 410 ml (14 fl oz) tins coconut milk (or use 3¼ cups (800 ml, 26 fl oz) freshly made)

~

2 tablespoons (60 g, 2 oz) red curry paste

~

8 chicken thighs, bones removed and flesh cut into 2 cm (¾ in) pieces

~

3 cups (750 ml, ¾ qt) water

~

1.5 kg (3 lb 4½ oz) pumpkin, peeled and cut into 4 cm (1½ in) chunks

~

⅔ cup (150 ml, 5 fl oz) Thai fish sauce (nam pla)

~

2 tablespoons white granulated sugar

~

salt to taste

~

6 Kaffir lime leaves, washed and torn

~

125 g (4 oz) pea eggplant (aubergine), stalk removed and washed (optional)

~

3 medium green chillies, washed and sliced on the diagonal

~

12 stalks Thai sweet basil, leaves removed and washed

~

3 red chillies for garnish

Heat the oil in a wok, then add 200 ml (7 fl oz) coconut milk. Simmer over medium high heat, stirring well, about 5 minutes. Add the curry paste, stir well to combine, simmering for another 5 minutes. Gradually pour in another 200 ml (7 fl oz) coconut milk, stirring all the time, then put in the chicken flesh. Combine well, then simmer gently for 15–20 minutes.

Meanwhile, in a large pot, combine 1 tin (410 ml, 14 fl oz) coconut milk with the water, bring to the boil and let simmer 5 minutes. Add chicken mixture to this, along with the pumpkin. Let simmer 10 minutes, then add remaining ingredients and simmer 20–30 minutes or until pumpkin and chicken are tender. Taste for sugar, salt and fish sauce. Garnish with red chillies which have been cut into flower shapes.

NOTE: Thai red curry paste can be purchased in tins from Asian food stores. Be sure to select a good-quality one.

Right: The pumpkin — the archetypal autumn vegetable.

STEAMED JASMINE RICE

JASMINE RICE IS AVAILABLE IN MOST ASIAN FOOD STORES AND SUPERMARKETS, OR YOU CAN USE AROMATIC THAI RICE.

INGREDIENTS

600 g (21 oz) jasmine rice

~

1¼ cups (300 ml, 10 fl oz) coconut milk

~

1¼ cups (300 ml, 10 fl oz) water

~

1 teaspoon sugar

~

½ teaspoon salt

~

¼ teaspoon cumin seeds

~

⅛ teaspoon saffron powder

Wash the rice under running water in a sieve. Combine well with the remaining ingredients in a medium-large saucepan.

Bring to the boil, then reduce heat and cook over very low heat, covered tightly, for 20 minutes. Remove from heat and let sit 10 minutes before serving.

Below: Steamed Jasmine Rice.

BLANCMANGER WITH RASPBERRY COULIS

~

THIS IS A SHIMMERING OLD-FASHIONED DESSERT. USE DR OETKER'S GELATINE LEAVES FOR
BEST RESULTS. YOU WILL FIND THIS BRAND IN GOOD DELICATESSENS.

INGREDIENTS

3 cups (500 g, 1 lb) blanched (skinned) almonds
~
6 bitter almonds (optional)
~
1¼ cups (300 ml, 10 fl oz) milk
~
⅔ cup (200 ml, 7 fl oz) water
~
extra milk
~
1½ cups (350 g, 12 oz) white granulated sugar
~
1¼ cups (300 ml, 10 fl oz) water
~
9 leaves gelatine or 6 teaspoons (20 g) powdered
~
3⅔ cups (900 ml, 30 fl oz) cream, whipped

Above: Blancmanger with Raspberry Coulis.

Put the almonds into an electric blender and blend until fine.
Scrape into a bowl and moisten with the milk and water.

Line a sieve with two layers of wet muslin (cheesecloth) and
put the almond paste into the muslin. Hang the sieve over a
bowl. Gather the bag together and squeeze hard to extract the
almond milk. You need 250 ml (8½ fl oz) of almond milk. Add
more milk to almond mixture to make up required amount.

Meanwhile, put the sugar and water together in a saucepan.
Heat gently over medium heat until the sugar is dissolved. Soak
the gelatine leaves in water to cover for 5 minutes, wring out,
and then add them to the warm sugar syrup. Stir well to dissolve.

When sugar syrup has cooled, combine with the almond milk.
(If using powdered gelatine, sprinkle the powder over the top of
the hot sugar syrup and whisk well to combine. Strain through a
sieve before adding to the almond milk.) Fold in the whipped
cream, and pour into 10 dariole moulds (small cylindrical moulds
— 200 ml (7 fl oz) capacity) which have been rinsed out with
water. Allow to set in the refrigerator. To turn out, dip the
moulds in warm water and turn upside down on to the serving
platter. Give them a good shake if necessary.

RASPBERRY COULIS

Put 300 g (10½ oz) fresh raspberries into an electric blender or
food processor with sugar to taste. Process until puréed, then
push through a sieve. Spoon onto plates after unmoulding the
blancmanger. This is nice served with some extra fresh berries.

PLATTER OF FRESH TROPICAL FRUITS

Choose from fruits in season and offer a selection on a platter
after the meal. Especially delicious served with a wedge of fresh
lime. In the photograph we used custard apple (cherimoya),
jackfruit, durian*, rambutans, feijoas (pineapple guava), pink and
white guavas and pink pawpaw (papaya). (See page 157 for a
key to the fruit.)
*NOTE: The durian is native to South-east Asia. The flavour of
the fruit is delicious but be warned — the fruit has a very strong
smell.

MENU

A Golden Roast Dinner

A more traditional English-style menu, featuring fowl, chestnuts and an elegant dessert.

GRILLED MUSHROOMS (FUNGHI ALLA GRIGLIA)

~

ROASTED SQUAB

~

CELERIAC PURÉE

~

CHESTNUTS

~

CARAMELISED ORANGES WITH SPUN SUGAR AND PISTACHIOS

~

ORANGE SORBET

Serves 6

GRILLED MUSHROOMS (FUNGHI ALLA GRIGLIA)

~

INGREDIENTS

750 g (1½ lb) fresh mushrooms

~

½ cup (125 ml, 4 fl oz) olive oil

~

flaky sea salt

~

pepper, freshly ground

~

1 large clove garlic, chopped

~

parsley, freshly chopped, preferably the Continental (flat-leaf) variety

~

chives, snipped

After wiping the mushrooms dry, place on a baking tray (sheet). Sprinkle with half the oil, the salt, pepper and chopped garlic. Marinate 5–10 minutes.

Place the mushrooms under the grill (broiler), about 12.5 cm (5 in) from the heat. Grill slowly, 6–8 minutes for larger ones, 4–5 minutes for smaller ones. If using oyster or enokitake mushrooms, allow 1–2 minutes, just to warm them through.

Serve on warm plates, sprinkled with chopped parsley, chives, remaining olive oil and pan juices.

ROASTED SQUAB

~

USE FRESH SQUAB IN THEIR PRIME. THEY SHOULD BE ROSY INSIDE, WITH THE JUICES RUNNING A LITTLE PINK.

INGREDIENTS

6 plump fresh squab

~

salt and pepper

~

olive oil

~

2 cups (500 ml, 17 fl oz) pigeon, veal or chicken stock

Preheat oven to 200°C (400°F). Wipe the squab dry and season with salt and pepper. Heat the oil in a frying pan (skillet) and seal the squab on all sides, two at a time, to crisp the skin. Roast in the preheated oven for 15–20 minutes. Remove and leave to rest in a warm place (wrapped in aluminium foil) 10–15 minutes.

Meanwhile, bring stock to boil on top of stove. Reduce to about 6 tablespoons.

To serve: remove legs and breast from squab and place onto warmed plates. Serve with a little of the reduced stock.

MUSHROOMS

Autumn is mushroom time. Choose a selection of cultivated ones from those available. Better still, pick your own (but be careful — wild mushrooms must be identified by a reputable source as there are many inedible and poisonous varieties).
Serve them as a warm salad. Wipe skins of larger mushrooms with a damp cloth to remove dirt and debris.
Trim the stem.
More delicate mushrooms like the oyster (shameji) or enokitake won't need wiping.

Previous page: Squab, Chestnuts and Celeriac.
Right: Grilled Mushrooms.

CELERIAC PURÉE

INGREDIENTS

1 large celeriac (celery root) (about 750 g, 26 oz), peeled and cut in chunks

~

2 golden delicious apples, peeled, cored and chopped

~

water or chicken stock

~

50–100 g (2–3 oz) butter, cut in pieces

~

juice of 1 small lemon or lime

~

salt, pepper, nutmeg

Cook the celeriac and apple together in sufficient water or chicken stock to barely cover. Simmer with lid off, until the celeriac is tender and the liquid evaporated.

Remove immediately to a food processor and process to a purée, feeding in the butter bit by bit. Add as much butter as you feel is required — celeriac has an uncanny capacity to take up a very large quantity.

Season with lemon or lime juice, salt and pepper and freshly grated nutmeg.

CHESTNUTS

THIS CAN BE PREPARED AHEAD AND REHEATED.

INGREDIENTS

12 brown eschallots, peeled

~

12 cloves garlic, peeled

~

olive oil

~

250 g (8 oz) kaiserfleisch (German bacon) or speck, sliced and cubed

~

1 small red (Spanish) onion, sliced then cut into half-moons

~

2 red apples, unpeeled, cored and cubed

~

500 g (1 lb) fresh chestnuts, cooked*

~

pepper and nutmeg

Preheat oven to 200°C (400°F). Roast the shallots and garlic in a little olive oil until golden and beginning to caramelise.

Film the bottom of a heavy frying pan (skillet) with olive oil, add the kaiserfleisch and cook until coloured. Add the onion and cook over gentle heat, about 15 minutes. Stir in the apples and cook until tender, about 10 minutes.

Combine with the chestnuts, roasted shallots and garlic. Serve as an accompaniment to squab.

*NOTE: To cook the chestnuts, boil them gently in a pan for 20 minutes. Drain and remove shells.

End of autumn.
The hop of a wild rabbit
Scuttling through dead leaves.

FLORENCE B. SPILGER, *NOVEMBER*

Left: The persimmon is a beautiful autumn
fruit — be sure to allow it to fully ripen before eating.

CARAMELISED ORANGES WITH SPUN SUGAR AND PISTACHIOS

INGREDIENTS

6–8 large oranges

~

2 tablespoons (40 ml) Grand Marnier (orange liqueur)

~

1 cup (250 g, 8 oz) white granulated sugar

~

½ cup (125 ml, 4 fl oz) water

~

2 tablespoons fresh pistachio nuts, peeled

Thinly pare the skin of 2 of the oranges and cut into fine shreds. Alternatively, use a zester. Blanch zest for 1 minute in boiling water, drain, dry on paper towels (absorbent kitchen paper) and set aside.

Peel the oranges, removing all white pith. Slice into rounds and place into a glass serving dish. Sprinkle with Grand Marnier.

Bring the sugar and water to the boil, heating gently until sugar dissolves. Boil, without stirring, over medium heat until the caramel is golden. Remove, then pour over the oranges, being careful of spluttering. Sprinkle with reserved orange zest and chill well. Just before serving, scatter over the pistachio nuts and top with the spun sugar.

SPUN SUGAR

INGREDIENTS

1 cup (250 g, 8 oz) white granulated sugar

~

100 ml (3½ fl oz) water

Put the sugar and water into a saucepan, heating gently until the sugar dissolves. Bring to boiling point and simmer over medium heat until it just begins to caramelise. Don't let it become dark.

Remove from heat. Dip two forks into the caramel, then hold them above the saucepan so that the syrup drips back into the pan. As the threads begin to thin out, pull them with your fingers, working quickly so that you don't get burnt (it is useful to wet your fingers before doing this). Wrap them around and around, then place on top of the oranges.

There is something in the autumn that is native to my blood —
Touch of manner, hint of mood;
And my heart is like a rhyme,
With the yellow and the purple and the crimson keeping time.

BLISS CARMAN, *A VAGABOND SONG*

Right: Caramelised Oranges with Spun Sugar and Pistachios; in the background Orange Sorbet.

ORANGE SORBET

INGREDIENTS

peel from 1 orange and 1 lemon or lime, finely pared

~

1½ cups (375 ml, 12 fl oz) water

~

1 cup (250 g, 8 oz) white granulated sugar

~

2⅓ cups (600 ml, 20 fl oz) orange juice, freshly squeezed

juice of 1 lime or lemon

Put the peel into a saucepan with the water and sugar and boil for 10 minutes. Strain and cool. Mix together with the orange and lime juice and stir well to combine. Freeze until the mixture starts to set, beat well and return to the freezer. Alternatively, pour into an ice-cream maker, churn and freeze. Remove from the freezer 15 minutes before serving.

WINTER

MENU

~

A Warming Winter Breakfast

Winter is the ideal season for hearty breakfasts. This menu takes advantage of the citrus fruits in season.

SEVILLE ORANGE MARMALADE

~

DIANA'S HEALTHY NO-KNEAD BREAD

~

FRUIT MUFFINS

~

ORANGE CURD

~

SCRAMBLED EGGS ON TOAST WITH RED CAVIAR

~

COMPOTE OF DRIED FRUITS WITH ORANGE BLOSSOM WATER

~

BLOOD ORANGE JUICE

Serves 6–8

SEVILLE ORANGE MARMALADE

INGREDIENTS

1.5 kg (3 lb) Seville (or bitter) oranges (about 8 medium)
~
12 cups (3 L, 3 qt) water
~
juice of 2 lemons
~
2.5 kg (5 lb) warmed white granulated sugar*

Previous page: In the foreground, Orange Curd; centre, Compote of Dried Fruits; in the background, Fruit Muffins.
Right: A variety of winter oranges.
Below: Seville Orange Marmalade.

Wash the fruit well and dry with a teatowel (dishcloth). Using a vegetable peeler, remove the orange zest as thinly as possible and cut into thin shreds. Put into a preserving pan with half the water and the lemon juice. Bring to the boil and simmer for 1½–2 hours or until peel is soft.

Meanwhile, cut the oranges (together with the pith) roughly and place in another pan with the remaining water. Add any seeds. Bring to the boil, cover with a lid and simmer 1½ hours.

Strain the orange pulp through a fine sieve or through muslin (cheesecloth) into the pan with the soft peel. Bring to the boil and reduce slightly. Add the warmed sugar. Boil rapidly until set. Ladle into sterilised jars and seal.

*NOTE: Warm the sugar in a tray in a moderate oven before adding — this helps it to dissolve more quickly.

DIANA'S HEALTHY NO-KNEAD BREAD

THIS BREAD IS BEST MADE WITH AN ELECTRIC MIXER AND REQUIRES NO KNEADING.
START WITH THE SMALLER QUANTITY OF WATER, ADDING MORE IF THE MIXTURE IS
TOO DRY. DO NOT PREHEAT THE OVEN.

INGREDIENTS

*4 cups (500 g, 1 lb) plain (all-purpose) stoneground
wholemeal (graham, wholewheat) flour*
~
½ cup (75 g, 2½ oz) gluten (strong or bread) flour
~
*½ cup (100 g, 3½ oz) mixed grains (millet, oats, ground
buckwheat)*
~
2 teaspoons dry (baker's) yeast
~
1 teaspoon salt
~
3–3½ cups (750–875 ml, 25–30 fl oz) warm water
~
2 teaspoons honey
~
1 tablespoon vegetable oil
~
handful sunflower seeds
~
extra wholemeal (graham, wholewheat) flour

Put the flour, gluten flour, mixed grains, yeast and salt into the mixing bowl and combine well. Add the water, honey and oil. Turn on the beaters and beat hard for two minutes until stringy and elastic.

Tip into a well-oiled bread tin (pan) and scatter with sunflower seeds and a little wholemeal flour. Cover with a teatowel (dishcloth) and let sit in a warm spot for 20 minutes. It won't look risen (proved) at this stage, but don't worry. Place the bread in the unheated oven and set at 220°C (425°F). Cook 40–45 minutes or until it feels hollow when tapped. Remove and let cool a little before removing from tin. If you like a crisp crust all over, return the bread to the hot oven for 8–10 minutes after removing from tin.

NOTE: Gluten flour is available from health food stores.

Before spring there are days like these:
Under the dense snow the meadow rests,
The trees merrily, drily rustle,
And the warm wind is tender and supple.
And the body marvels at its lightness,
And you don't recognise your own house,
And that song you were tired of before,
You sing like a new one, with deep emotion.

ANNA AKHMATOVA

Left: Diana's Healthy No-knead Bread.

FRUIT MUFFINS

INGREDIENTS

1 cup (125 g, 4 oz) plain (all-purpose) flour

~

1 cup (125 g, 4 oz) wholemeal (graham, wholewheat flour)

~

2 teaspoons baking powder

~

pinch salt

~

¼ cup (60 g, 2 oz) white granulated sugar

~

2 eggs

~

½ cup (125 ml, 4 fl oz) milk, soured with a squeeze of lemon

~

125 g (4 oz) melted butter

~

125–150 g (4–5 oz) mixed fruit and nuts (currants, sultanas (golden raisins), dates, dried apricots, figs, fresh apples and bananas, almonds, pecans and walnuts) chopped into small pieces

Butter and flour 12 muffin tins (pans). Preheat oven to 200°C (400°F).

Sift together the flours, baking powder, salt and sugar. In another bowl, beat the eggs and add the milk and melted butter. Add the liquid to the dry ingredients with a few swift strokes. Add fruit and nuts at this stage, if using. Be careful not to overmix as this will develop the gluten in the flour and make the muffins tough. The ingredients should be just combined. Spoon into prepared muffin tins and bake 20–25 minutes. Serve warm.

Makes 12 medium or 8 large muffins

ORANGE CURD

INGREDIENTS

4 oranges

~

125 g (4 oz) unsalted (sweet) butter, chopped

~

6 eggs

~

½ cup (125 g, 4 oz) white granulated sugar

Wash the oranges, dry well, and remove the zest with a zester (peeler). Squeeze the juice. Combine the zest and juice with the remaining ingredients in the top of a double boiler, or place in a bowl over a pan of gently simmering water.

Heat slowly, whisking from time to time to combine. When the mixture has thickened and coats the back of a spoon, remove from heat and push through a sieve. Spoon into sterilised jars. Store in the refrigerator. The Orange Curd will keep 2–3 weeks.

Winter lingered so long in the lap of Spring, that it occasioned a great deal of talk.

BILL NYE, *SPRING*

Right: The making of muffins.

SCRAMBLED EGGS ON TOAST WITH RED CAVIAR

ALLOW 2 EGGS AND 1 TABLESPOON (20 ML) MILK PER PERSON, PLUS A GOOD
DESSERTSPOON OF CAVIAR.

INGREDIENTS

2 eggs
~
1 tablespoon (20 ml) (single, light) cream or milk
~
salt and pepper
~
knob of butter
~
2 slices toast
~
1 teaspoon red lumpfish 'caviar'

Beat together the eggs with the cream or milk and a pinch of salt and pepper.

Melt the butter in a pan, pour in the eggs and cook over low heat, stirring until eggs are creamy and soft.

Serve immediately over pieces of hot buttered toast, with the caviar spooned on top.

COMPOTE OF DRIED FRUITS WITH ORANGE BLOSSOM WATER

THIS DELICIOUS COMPOTE KEEPS WELL IN THE REFRIGERATOR FOR A WEEK OR
MORE. USE ORANGE BLOSSOM WATER TO TASTE. DIFFERENT BRANDS HAVE DIFFERENT
STRENGTHS. IT SHOULD ADD A LINGERING FRAGRANCE TO THE DISH.

INGREDIENTS

500 g (1 lb) mixed dried fruits (apricots, prunes, pears, figs, peaches)
~
water to cover
~
½ cup (110 g, 3½ oz) caster (superfine) sugar
~
peeled rind of 1 large orange
~
6 cloves
~
2 star anise
~
1 cinnamon stick
~
orange blossom water to taste

Put the dried fruits into a medium-large saucepan and just cover with water. Add the sugar, rind and whole spices. Bring to the boil, stirring to dissolve the sugar. Turn heat down and let simmer gently 25–30 minutes or until the fruits are swollen and are beginning to soften.

Remove from heat and let cool. Add the orange blossom water, a few drops to begin with, and stir well. Taste and add more if necessary — be careful not to overdo it. Chill well before serving.

Right: Scrambled Eggs on Toast with Red Caviar and Blood Orange Juice.

BLOOD ORANGE JUICE

Blood oranges come into season towards the end of winter. Their colour is glorious, and they make a marvellous juice when squeezed.

MENU

An Earthy Winter Lunch

Cabbage and parsnips are vegetables which are often overlooked. The delicious Cabbage Rolls, the focus of this menu, are richly flavoured with tomatoes, white wine and yoghurt.

PEAR AND PARSNIP SOUP

~

BREAD ROLLS

~

CABBAGE ROLLS

~

POACHED QUINCES WITH BLACK RICE PUDDING
AND COCONUT CREAM

Serves 6

PEAR AND PARSNIP SOUP

INGREDIENTS

3 soft yellow faultless pears (about 650 g, 22 oz)

~

2–3 parsnips (about 425 g, 14½ oz), creamy in colour

~

6 cups (1.5 L, 1½ qt) chicken stock

~

salt and white pepper

~

½ cup (125 ml, 4 fl oz) (single, light) cream

~

extra whipped cream and watercress for garnishing

Peel and core the pears. Peel and chop the parsnips. Put into a saucepan and cover with 2 cups (500 ml, 17 fl oz) of the stock. Bring to the boil, then simmer gently until tender. Blend in a food processor until smooth.

Return to heat, add remaining chicken stock, salt and white pepper and simmer gently for about 15 minutes. Just before serving, stir through cream.

Garnish with a peak of whipped cream and sprig of watercress.

Previous page: Poached Quinces with Black Rice Pudding and Coconut Cream.

BREAD ROLLS

THESE ROLLS ARE DELICIOUS SERVED WITH THE PEAR AND PARSNIP SOUP. YOU WILL NEED TO START MAKING THEM IN THE MORNING.

INGREDIENTS

6 cups (750 g, 25 oz) unbleached white bread (strong) flour

~

1½ teaspoons salt

~

2½ teaspoons dry (baker's) yeast

~

2 cups (500 ml, 17 fl oz) lukewarm water

~

¼ teaspoon sugar

~

2 tablespoons vegetable oil

~

poppy seeds or sesame seeds

Put the flour and salt into a large warmed bowl. Run your fingers through the flour and salt to combine well. Make a well in the centre.

In a separate bowl, put the yeast and ½ cup (125 ml, 4 fl oz) of the water. Add the sugar and stir well to combine. Let stand 5–10 minutes to activate the yeast.

Pour the yeast mixture into the well in the centre of the flour and add the remaining water, which should be at blood temperature. Mix together the flour and liquid with your fingers, then beat with your hand, adding more water if needed to make a firm dough.

Turn out onto a well-floured bench and slap it around until it begins to feel elastic. Knead the dough by pushing it firmly away from you with the heel of your hand, turning the dough a little at a time. Repeat. Continue kneading until the dough is smooth and elastic and springs back when you make a dent in it with your finger. Put it into a clean, warm, oiled bowl, cover with oiled plastic (cling) wrap and a cloth. Leave to rise (prove) in a warm place for an hour or more. You will know it is ready when a finger pushed into the dough leaves an indentation. Knock back (punch down) the dough a few times to push out any large bubbles. Turn onto a lightly floured board and knead three or four times.

Pat the dough out into a rectangle and cut into 18–20 equal parts. Shape into thick rounds, turning under to make balls; or roll out into a sausage shape and twist into a knot. Place the rolls on a lightly oiled baking tray (sheet), sprinkle with poppy or sesame seeds and cover with oiled plastic (cling) wrap and a cloth. Leave in a warm place until almost doubled in bulk. This will take between 1–2 hours. Preheat the oven to 200°C (400°F) and cook 20–25 minutes or until the rolls sound hollow when tapped underneath.

Opposite page: Pear and Parsnip Soup with Bread Rolls.
Left: The bounty of winter.

CABBAGE ROLLS

~

USE HEADING OR PEKING (CHINESE) CABBAGE FOR THESE DELICIOUS ROLLS.

INGREDIENTS

1 large cabbage

~

1 onion, finely chopped

~

1 celery stalk, chopped

~

2 garlic cloves, crushed

~

1 tablespoon (20 mls) vegetable oil

~

375 g (13 oz) minced (ground) round steak

~

375 g (13 oz) minced (ground) lean pork

~

1 cup (150 g, 5 oz) cooked rice

~

2 tablespoons parsley, chopped

~

1 teaspoon each paprika and ground cumin

~

salt and pepper to taste

~

1 tablespoon watercress, chopped (optional)

~

juice and zest ½ lemon

~

2 egg yolks

~

60 g (2 oz) butter

~

1 tablespoon plain (all-purpose) flour

~

1 cup (250 ml, 8 oz) tomatoes, peeled and chopped

~

½ cup (125 ml, 4 fl oz) white wine

~

bay (laurel) leaf

~

¾ cup (185 ml, 6 oz) natural (plain) yoghurt or (dairy) sour cream

Preheat oven to 180°C (350°F).

Separate the leaves carefully from the cabbage and choose 12–14 large ones. Cut off the hard stalks at the bottom. Bring a large pan of water to the boil, throw in the leaves and blanch for a few minutes. Remove and refresh under cold water.

Spread the leaves out on teatowels (dishcloths) or paper towels (absorbent kitchen paper) to dry.

In a frying pan (skillet), sauté the onion, celery and garlic in the oil until soft.

Put the meat into a bowl and mix in the rice, parsley, paprika, cumin, salt and pepper, watercress, lemon juice and zest, egg yolks and the cooked onion, celery and garlic. Combine well. Spoon the mixture evenly into each cabbage leaf. Roll up, tucking in the sides, and secure with toothpicks.

Melt the butter in a frying pan, and sauté the cabbage rolls a few at a time until golden, turning occasionally. Transfer to a baking dish. Stir the flour into the juices from the frying pan, mix well and bring to simmering point. Add the tomatoes and wine, bay leaf and yoghurt or sour cream. Pour over the cabbage rolls. Cover and bake in the preheated oven for an hour.

Makes 12–14

Right: Cabbage Rolls.
Opposite page: The cabbage is one of the most widely cultivated vegetables.

POACHED QUINCES WITH BLACK RICE PUDDING AND COCONUT CREAM

INGREDIENTS

6 quinces, each weighing approximately 325–350 g (12 oz)

~

8 cups (2 L, 2 qt) water

~

3 cups (750 g, 26 oz) white granulated sugar

~

2 star anise

~

6 cardamom pods, bruised

~

juice of 3 lemons

Rub the fur off the quinces and wash well. Put them into a pot, packed fairly tightly, together with the water and sugar. Add the star anise and cardamom pods. Bring to the boil and simmer briskly uncovered for up to 2½–3 hours, turning a few times during the cooking.

Add the juice of the lemons during the last stages of cooking and turn the temperature down to prevent the jelly catching. You may need to use a simmer pad to stop any burning.

To serve, remove the quinces from the pot and slice into halves. Drizzle with the delicious pink syrup in which they were cooked.

BLACK RICE PUDDING

THIS PUDDING, WHICH SOME CALL 'BLACK ANT' PUDDING, HAS THE UNMISTAKABLE FLAVOUR AND AROMA OF THE EAST. IF YOU CAN'T FIND PALM SUGAR, SUBSTITUTE SOFT, LIGHT BROWN SUGAR. BLACK RICE IS AVAILABLE IN ASIAN FOOD STORES.

INGREDIENTS

1½ cups (250 g, 8 oz) black (unpolished, sticky) rice (japonica), washed and soaked overnight

~

4 cups (1 L, 1 qt) water

~

¾ cup (125 g, 4 oz) palm sugar

~

garnish: coconut cream and shredded (flaked) coconut

Soak the rice overnight in enough cold water to cover. Drain well, washing with plenty of water as you do so. Put the rice into a large saucepan, add the water and bring to the boil. Simmer gently for 30–40 minutes, uncovered, then add the palm sugar and cook another 20–25 minutes, or until the rice is soft. It should be thick and the rice soft but firm.

Serve with a little coconut cream poured over the top and garnish with shredded coconut.

...cabbage my poem
food of our forefathers
garden of the cellar's long winter

a green rose
you lie composed
quiet and closed as a tomb

KATE LLEWELLYN, *CABBAGE* (excerpt)

Right: The quince is an under-appreciated winter fruit — it has a tart, astringent flavour.

MENU

A Depths of Winter Dinner

This is the classic cold weather dinner, featuring all the traditional roast dinner trimmings.

LEEKS VINAIGRETTE

~

STANDING RIB ROAST WITH RED WINE BUTTER SAUCE

~

ROASTED ROSEMARY POTATOES

~

STEAMED BABY VEGETABLES

~

ROAST ONIONS

~

STICKY DATE PUDDING WITH BUTTERSCOTCH SAUCE

~

CANDIED ORANGE AND CITRON PEEL

~

CHOCOLATE TRUFFLES

Serves 8–10

LEEKS VINAIGRETTE

THESE LEEKS, FLAVOURED WITH A MINT VINAIGRETTE, MAKE A DELICIOUS AND REFRESHING START TO THE MEAL.

INGREDIENTS

Allow 3–4 baby leeks per person

VINAIGRETTE

½ cup (125 ml, 4 fl oz) olive oil

~

1½ tablespoons (30 ml) white wine vinegar

~

1 garlic clove, crushed

~

salt and pepper to taste

~

2 tablespoons fresh mint, chopped

Cut off all but about 5 cm (2 in) of the green tops of the leeks, cutting to a point so that you retain the tender inner part. Slice off the roots and wash thoroughly under running water to ensure that all the grit is removed. You can also slit the leeks in half lengthways to about 2.5 cm (1 in) of the root end and then wash them.

Put the leeks into a steamer and steam over simmering water for 10–15 minutes or until they are tender. Remove and refresh under cold water. Drain and place on serving plates. Spoon a little vinaigrette dressing over the leeks and serve immediately.

VINAIGRETTE

Combine all the ingredients and mix well.

STANDING RIB ROAST

INGREDIENTS

1 standing best rib roast, 4–5 ribs

~

2 garlic cloves, peeled and cut into slivers

~

salt and freshly ground black pepper

Ask the butcher to prepare a standing rib roast: 4–5 ribs will be ample. Ask for meat which has been well aged. It should be a rich red to dark red colour. The best rib meat comes from the fore rib, nearest the loin.

Preheat oven to 250°C (500°F). Season the meat with salt and freshly ground black pepper and insert a few slivers of garlic in between the ribs. Cover the rib tips with aluminium foil, shiny side in, to prevent burning. When oven is hot, put in the meat, standing upright on a lightly oiled roasting pan. Cook 20 minutes, then turn down heat to 180°C (350°F). Continue to roast, basting occasionally with pan juices.

Allow approximately 15 minutes per 500 g (1 lb) for rare meat, 20 minutes per 500 g for medium and 25 minutes per 500 g for well-done. Alternatively, you can use a meat thermometer. Remove beef from pan and reserve juice for Red Wine Sauce (see page 141). It is very important to allow the meat to rest for 25–30 minutes in a warm place, covered with aluminium foil, before you start carving. This allows the juices to settle.

Previous page: Standing Rib Roast, Roasted Rosemary Potatoes, Roast Onions and Steamed Baby Vegetables.
Right: Leeks Vinaigrette.

ROAST ROSEMARY POTATOES AND ROAST ONIONS

INGREDIENTS

8–10 medium potatoes

~

freshly chopped rosemary

~

salt

Cook the potatoes in a separate baking dish. Allow 1–2 potatoes per person, depending on their size. Peel them and cut into chunks. Heat 2–3 tablespoons oil in a baking dish, toss in the potatoes and scatter with freshly chopped rosemary. Season with salt and put into the oven with the meat. Turn the potatoes from time to time. If they need crisping at the end, turn up the oven to hot whilst meat is resting — this will ensure they are crisp and golden.

ROAST ONIONS

Peel 10 baby onions and add to the roast potatoes. Proceed as for potatoes, above.

STEAMED BABY VEGETABLES

INGREDIENTS

40 baby carrots, scraped

~

20 baby turnips, peeled if necessary, leaves on

Steam the baby vegetables in a wok over simmering water until tender. Alternatively, plunge them into boiling salted water until just tender, then remove and refresh quickly under cold water.

RED WINE BUTTER SAUCE

INGREDIENTS

1 onion, finely chopped

~

2 cups (500 ml, 16 fl oz) red wine

~

4 cups (1 L, 1 qt) beef stock

~

salt and pepper, to taste

~

knob of butter, about 20 g ($^2/_3$ oz)

After the beef has been removed from the roasting pan, sauté the onion in the juices and fat from the beef on top of the stove.

Pour the red wine into the pan and reduce by half. Pour in the beef stock and boil rapidly for 2–3 minutes. Put through a sieve into a clean saucepan and skim the fat from the top of the stock. Bring back to the boil and reduce by two-thirds, correcting seasoning. Whisk the knob of butter into the sauce just before serving.

Left: Perhaps the best loved vegetable of them all — the adaptable, nutritious potato.

STICKY DATE PUDDING

INGREDIENTS

2½ cups (400 g, 14 oz) pitted dates

~

juice and zest of 1 orange

~

approximately 2 cups (500 ml, 17 fl oz) water

~

2 teaspoons baking powder

~

125 g (4 oz) unsalted (sweet) butter

~

½ cup (90 g, 3 oz) soft, light brown sugar

~

½ cup (110 g, 3½ oz) caster (superfine) sugar

~

1 teaspoon vanilla essence (extract)

~

4 eggs

~

3 cups (375 g, 13½ oz) self-raising flour

Lightly grease 8–10 x 200 ml (7 fl oz) dariole moulds. Preheat oven to 180°C (350°F).

Put the dates into a saucepan. Pour the orange juice into a measuring jug (cup) and bring up to 2 cups (500 ml, 17 fl oz) with water. Pour over the dates. Add the zest, bring to the boil and gently simmer until the dates are soft. Remove the mixture from the heat and cool. Stir in the baking powder.

Beat the butter until soft, then add the sugars and cream until light and fluffy. Add the vanilla and eggs one at a time. Add the date mixture and combine well. Fold through the sifted flour. Spoon the mixture into dariole moulds — the mixture should come about two-thirds of the way up.

Cover each pudding tightly with aluminium foil. Stand the puddings on a baking tray (sheet) and pour some boiling water into the tray (enough to come ⅓ of the way up the sides of the puddings). Cook in the preheated oven 1 hour 15 minutes, or until a skewer inserted in the centre comes out clean.

BUTTERSCOTCH SAUCE

INGREDIENTS

250 g (8 oz) unsalted (sweet) butter

~

2½ cups (400 g, 14 oz) soft, light brown sugar

~

1 cup (250 ml, 8 fl oz) (single, light) cream

Melt the butter, add the sugar and stir until sugar has dissolved. Pour in the cream, bring to the boil and simmer until sauce is smooth.

When one end of the Milky Way drops it is time to put on wadded clothes.

CHINESE PROVERB

Left: Sticky Date Pudding with Butterscotch Sauce.

CANDIED ORANGE PEEL

YOU CAN USE GRAPEFRUIT, LEMONS, LIMES, CITRON OR ORANGES WHEN MAKING THIS
GLORIOUS TRANSLUCENT SWEET.

INGREDIENTS

peel of 6 oranges

~

4 cups (1 kg, 2 lb 3 oz) white granulated sugar

~

2 cups (500 ml, 17 fl oz) water

~

caster (superfine) sugar (optional)

Wash the oranges and peel them thickly. When peeling, include the white pith which clings to the outer skin as it turns translucent in the syrup.

Boil the peel in plenty of water until tender. Drain and boil again in fresh water for 20 minutes.

Bring the sugar and water to the boil, stirring to make sure the sugar is dissolved. Put in the peel and boil until syrup has almost disappeared, stirring to prevent burning. A simmer pad is useful in the last stages.

Remove the peel from saucepan and spread on baking trays (sheets) lined with non-stick baking paper and leave to dry in the sun. Or dry it out in a cool oven (about 50°C (130°F)) for 30–45 minutes. Be careful not to overdry.

The peel can be rolled in caster sugar, if desired. Store in airtight jars.

CHOCOLATE TRUFFLES

INGREDIENTS

200 ml (7 fl oz) (single, light) cream

~

*250 g (8 oz) dark (plain or semi-sweet) chocolate,
chopped roughly*

~

3 teaspoons (10 g, ⅓ oz) unsalted (sweet) butter, chopped

~

3 teaspoons (15 ml) dark rum

~

good-quality cocoa, sifted

Bring the cream to the boil. Put the chocolate into a bowl and pour the cream over, stirring until chocolate has melted and is smooth. Stir in the butter and when cool, add the rum. Put into the refrigerator and allow to set. When almost set, remove from refrigerator and form mixture into small balls, approximately 10–12 g (⅓ oz) each. You can use a piping bag with a plain nozzle to do this, or a teaspoon. Place the balls on a tray lined with non-stick baking paper and return to the refrigerator until firm. Remove and toss in cocoa.

Makes 28

Right: Candied Orange Peel and Chocolate Truffles.

MENU

After an Opening — A Winter Supper

A casual affair, in which guests help themselves to the food displayed on tables and sideboard. All the preparation can be done ahead so you don't have to rush back from the theatre or art gallery and start cooking.

LEG OF PROSCIUTTO

~

PLATTER OF OYSTERS

~

TABLE OF CHEESES, OLIVES, DRIED FRUITS AND NUTS

~

GOAT'S CHEESE TARTS

~

DILL SCONES (BISCUITS) WITH A SIDE OF SMOKED SALMON, SOUR CREAM AND CHAMPAGNE

~

PANFORTE

Serves 25–30

LEG OF PROSCIUTTO WITH PLATTER OF OYSTERS

Prosciutto (or Parma ham) is the fine quality raw ham which originated in Parma, Italy. To serve, slice very
thinly and place on crusty bread with unsalted (sweet) butter.
A platter of freshly shucked oysters, dressed at the last minute with a little freshly squeezed lemon juice, is
always a treat. Choose local oysters in season and store in the refrigerator on crushed ice, covered with
plastic (cling) wrap.

TABLE OF CHEESES, OLIVES, DRIED FRUITS AND NUTS

Set out a spread of cheeses and dried fruits for guests to help themselves.
In our photograph, we have used a selection of delicious soft Italian cheeses: in the foreground, stracchino (a
rindless soft white cheese with a tangy flavour); left, a wheel of fresh ricotta (dill on top); centre, a baked
ricotta; and top, Mascarpone Reale (a mixture of mascarpone with gorgonzola, studded with walnuts).
Like the oysters and prosciutto, these are best served with crusty fresh bread.

Previous page: Leg of Prosciutto and Platter of Oysters.
Above: Winter is the season for citrus fruits — grapefruit, lemons and limes.
Right: Table of Cheeses, Olives, Dried Fruits and Nuts.

GOAT'S CHEESE TARTS

INSPIRED BY A RECIPE OF JOSEPHINE PIGNOLET.

INGREDIENTS

PASTRY

2⅓ cups (300 g, 10½ oz) plain (all-purpose) flour

~

a good pinch of salt

~

270 g (9 oz) cold butter

~

¼ cup (60–70 ml, 2–2½ fl oz) iced water

FILLING

3 eggs

~

½ onion, finely chopped

~

½ garlic clove, finely chopped

~

2 teaspoons olive oil

~

1¼ cups (300 ml, 10½ fl oz) (single, light) cream

~

*a handful of chopped fresh herbs — sorrel, spinach or
parsley, chopped rosemary, sage, etc.*

~

2 sprigs of thyme, leaves only

~

1 bay (laurel) leaf

~

pinch of nutmeg

~

salt and pepper to taste

~

*100 g (3 oz) chèvre cheese (goat's milk cheese), rind removed
and sliced into 24–30 rounds*

Put the flour onto a work surface with the salt. Using a hand grater, grate the butter over the flour and toss lightly together. Rub the butter into the flour with your fingertips, moistening with the water and using the heel of your hand, smear the pastry into a reasonably smooth mass. Wrap in plastic (cling) wrap and refrigerate for 30 minutes before rolling. Roll out the pastry and line 24–30 small pastry cases — the number you make will depend on the size of the individual moulds.

Preheat oven to 210°C (400°F). Press aluminium foil over the pastry and weight down with pastry weights or baking beans. Bake for 10–15 minutes, remove foil and weights. Reduce oven heat to 180°C (350°F) and return shells to oven to dry out the pastry.

FILLING

Preheat oven to 180°C (350°F).

Beat the eggs well.

Sweat the onion and garlic in the olive oil along with the sorrel, if it's being used. Bring the cream to the boil, then add the onions and herbs, thyme leaves, bay leaf and seasonings. Add the cream mixture to the beaten eggs at boiling point. Mix together well, but don't beat with the whisk.

Place the precooked pastry cases on baking trays (sheets) and place in the preheated oven — this makes it easier to pour in the filling. Check the seasonings before pouring the mixture into the shells. Place the slices of chèvre carefully on the top of each tart. Bake for 10–15 minutes, or until filling has set.

Makes 24–30

Right: Goat's Cheese Tarts.

Dill Scones (Biscuits) with a Side of Smoked Salmon, Sour Cream and Champagne

THERE ARE SOME CLASSIC COMBINATIONS WHICH NEVER FAIL — IN THIS CASE, SMOKED SALMON WITH SOUR CREAM AND CHAMPAGNE.

INGREDIENTS

3 cups (375 g, 12 oz) plain (all-purpose) white flour
~
3 cups (375 g, 12 oz) plain (all-purpose) wholemeal (graham, wholewheat) flour
~
pinch salt
~
125 g (4 oz) unsalted (sweet) butter, softened
~
2 cups (500 ml, 16 fl oz) milk, soured with the juice of ½ lemon
~
3 tablespoons dill, freshly chopped
~
extra milk, if required
~
2 cups (500 ml, 16 fl oz) (dairy) sour cream
~
smoked salmon
~
bunch fresh dill, for garnishing

Preheat the oven to 200°C (400°F).

Sift the flours and salt into a large bowl. With your fingertips, rub through the butter until the mixture resembles breadcrumbs. Make a well in the centre and stir in the milk. Add the dill. With your hands, bring the mixture gently together, adding more milk if necessary. Tip out onto a floured bench and pat out into a rectangle.

Cut out scone (biscuit) shapes with a scone cutter or up-turned glass dipped in flour, and place close together on a greased baking tray (sheet). Keep reshaping the dough as you go. Brush the tops of the scones with milk and dust with a little extra flour. Bake 20–25 minutes or until the scones have risen and are golden.

Allow to cool, then split in half. Spread each half with some sour cream, top with a generous piece of smoked salmon and more freshly chopped dill.

Makes 18–20 large scones

when I move house
the first tree I plant
is a lemon

biblical
sour and versatile
I much prefer it
to those cloying salesgirls
the soft stone fruits

KATE LLEWELLYN, *LEMON* (excerpt)

Left: Dill Scones (Biscuits) with a Side of Smoked Salmon and Sour Cream.

PANFORTE

~

THIS NOUGAT-LIKE CAKE, RICH IN NUTS AND FRUIT, IS A SPECIALITY OF SIENA IN ITALY. IF YOU CAN'T FIND RICE PAPER, USE ALUMINIUM FOIL BRUSHED LIGHTLY WITH OIL.

INGREDIENTS

2 cups (250 g, 8 oz) hazelnuts

~

2 cups (250 g, 8 oz) macadamia nuts

~

1½ cups (250 g, 8 oz) dried figs, chopped

~

1 cup (125 g, 4 oz) glacé (candied) apricots, chopped

~

1 cup (125 g, 4 oz) glacé (candied) pears, chopped

~

¾ cup (125 g, 4 oz) raisins

~

¾ cup (125 g, 4 oz) mixed (candied) peel

~

2 cups (250 g, 8 oz) plain (all-purpose) flour

~

1 tablespoon cinnamon

~

1 teaspoon nutmeg

~

¾ cup (300 ml, 10 fl oz) honey

~

1½ cups (300 g, 10 oz) caster (superfine) sugar

~

rice paper

Roast the nuts in a moderate oven (180°C (350°F)) until golden. Allow to cool, then rub the skins off the hazelnuts and put into a bowl with the roughly chopped fruits, flour and spices. Combine well.

Put the honey and sugar into a saucepan and bring to the boil until it reaches the soft ball stage (112–116°C (234–240°F))*. Pour over the fruit and nut mixture and stir well to combine. It will be very sticky and you may need to use your hands.

Heat the oven to 150°C (300°F). Line a 30 x 24 x 2.5 cm (12 x 9½ x 1 in) baking tray (sheet) with rice paper and press the mixture into the tray. Flatten the top. If you dip your hands in milk, this will help. Put another layer of rice paper over the top, pressing down well, and place in the oven. Cook for 45 minutes. Turn out to cool and cut into squares or large rectangles. Store in airtight containers.

* To determine soft ball stage — drop a small quantity of the honey and sugar mixture into a glass of iced water. If it forms a ball which flattens but does not disintegrate between your fingers, it has reached soft ball stage.

We give thanks for the blessing of winter:
Season to cherish the heart.
To make warmth and quiet for the heart.
To make soups and broths for the heart.
To cook for the heart and read for the heart.
To curl up softly and nestle with the heart.
To sleep deeply and gently at one with the heart.
To dream with the heart.
To spend time with the heart.
A long, long time of peace with the heart.
We give thanks for the blessing of winter:
Season to cherish the heart.
Amen

MICHAEL LEUNIG, *THE PRAYER TREE*

Right: Panforte.

POETRY ACKNOWLEDGMENTS

Pages v, 54, Rainer Maria Rilke from *The Selected Poetry of Rainer Maria Rilke* by Stephen Mitchell, translator. Copyright © 1982 by Stephen Mitchell. Reprinted by permission of Random House Inc, New York and Pan Books Ltd, London.

Page 18, Ki no Tsurayuki from Kenneth Rexroth: *One Hundred More Poems from the Japanese.* Copyright ©1974, 1976 by Kenneth Rexroth. Reprinted by permission of New Directions Publishing Corp., New York.

Page 31, Csezlaw Milosz, *Gift*, Ecco Press Inc, New York.

Pages 64, 154, taken from *The Prayer Tree*, © Michael Leunig. Used with permission. Collins Dove, Melbourne.

Page 123, 'Before spring there are days like these...' by Anna Akhmatova is translated by Judith Hemschemeyer, and is reprinted from *The Complete Poems of Anna Akhmatova* (second edition, 1992) with the permission of Zephyr Press of Somerville, Massachusetts, USA. Translation copyright © 1990, 1992 by Judith Hemschemeyer.

156

NOTES

PHOTO KEY

1. Custard apple (cherimoya)
2. Jackfruit
3. Durian
4. Rambutan
5. Feijoa (pineapple guava)
6. Pink guava
7. White guava
8. Pink pawpaw (papaya)
9. Carambola
10. Kiwano

OVEN TEMPERATURES AND GAS MARKS

Deg (C)	110	120	140	150	160	180	190	200	220	230	240	260
Deg (F)	225	250	275	300	325	350	375	400	425	450	475	500
Gas Mark	¼	½	1	2	3	4	5	6	7	8	9	10

A NOTE ON MEASUREMENTS

Metric and imperial weights and cup and spoon measures are provided for all ingredient quantities. A 250 ml (8 fl oz) cup has been used.

INDEX